Diaries of Doing Time
until the ICE Men Cometh

Diaries of Doing Time until the ICE Men Cometh

Philip M Jones

ATHENA PRESS
LONDON

Diaries of Doing Time until the ICE Men Cometh
Copyright © Philip M Jones 2007

All Rights Reserved

ISBN 10-digit: 1 84748 093 4
ISBN 13-digit: 978 1 84748 093 4

First Published 2007 by
ATHENA PRESS
Queen's House, 2 Holly Road
Twickenham TW1 4EG
United Kingdom

Printed for Athena Press

The events recounted in these pages are real; some names
have been changed.

Preface

Memories of Metropolitan Correctional Center (MCC) and Corrections Corporation of America (CCA) will be in my mind, heart and soul for the remainder of my life, just as my home country of Wales will always hold a place in my heart. I have a strong character, so I came out to freedom relatively unscathed. I also had a strong desire to tell others my stories of life inside as a prisoner, and to present an informed, unbiased, factual point of view of the American prison system, which I got to know so well in a relatively short time. This book is also about the people that I met and got to know well. I came to see, on a daily basis, what a waste of human life it is to be incarcerated because of the mistakes of life. There has to be a better way of effecting justice than keeping a human being in a prison warehouse system for profit.

The Brecon Beacons, Wales

Acknowledgements

I would like to thank everybody that has helped me to publish my book: first and foremost, Linda in California, who helped in so many ways so that I could have a life to start all over again in Great Britain; also Tricia, Tom and Natalie for all your help while I was in MCC and CCA; the Burnham Institute for allowing me to work in such an interesting, challenging environment every day, unaware that I was an illegal alien in the United States of America. Thanks to Pete and Gail for your references used in court in San Diego; also to my niece, Philippa, and her husband, Richard, for the references that you also supplied for the court.

To my long-time friends of over twenty years, Gren and Moira, for your love and support over all these past years, thank you. To all the libraries in Richmond, Twickenham and Whitton where I spent so many hours working on the computers for the book, thank you for being there. To Bev.gov in Cardiff, Wales, thank you for all your help.

I would also like to thank Travel Care in Heathrow Airport for giving me such a warm welcome and a cup of tea when I arrived back in Great Britain after so many years away. I would like to thank all the staff at Prisoners Abroad, especially Theresa, for all your help; some of the proceeds of this book will be donated to help the many more expats who arrive daily here in the United Kingdom from all over the world. I hope that you continue your work to help them all in so many ways.

A special thanks to my publisher, all your staff and the very creative design department. Thanks also go to friends in Wales.

Please email me any comments regarding my book; I would be interested to hear your honest opinion – good or not so good. Thank you for buying the book.

Philip M Jones
iamphilmJ@yahoo.com

Contents

Life in Great Britain

On May 5th every year in Mexico and California there is a celebration called *Cinco de Mayo*. It commemorates the victory of Hispanic nationals over the invading French at the battle of Puebla in 1862. This is the date I was born: on May 5th in the year of our Lord 1957. Of course, at that time and in the following years, I would never have thought how I would be associated and living with 210 Mexican people under one roof, or with asylum seekers from all over the world.

I was born in Church Village, South Glamorgan, in Wales to Raymond and Nancy Jones. My parents died when I was a child: my father first, taken by a brain haemorrhage when I was eleven, and then my mother, passing of thyroid cancer when I was fifteen. After her death, my family thought it was best that I started work, and so I moved to Cardiff, the capital of Wales, to live with my brother.

I worked as a motor mechanic for a number of years and met Martyn. He introduced me to a friend of his in London, where I moved in 1982. He was the manager of a private sports club called The Exiles Club. This club was run for the employees of Cable & Wireless.

Life in Spain and the American Connection

After a few years of hard work in London, I wanted to travel and decided to emigrate to southern Spain. I had visited Fuengirola and Marbella many times for vacations and thought that I would like to live and work in the country.

In January 1987 I arrived at Malaga Airport. I had reserved a small Fiat Panda rental car from Los Boliches car hire and drove the car to Fuengirola, where I had reserved a room at Hostel Italia. I also opened a Spanish bank account at the local Banco Central and transferred funds from London to Spain. I used the funds as a weekly living allowance, but found that I still needed to get a job locally.

This is where I found Salon Varietés – a little English-run theatre in Fuengirola. They gave me a job setting up props and scenery for the different productions put on in Spanish and English. It was fun work.

I also wanted to use my time in Spain to travel to Morocco, Portugal and Gibraltar. I decided that the best way to do this was to purchase a car and, in an English paper called *SUR,* I came across a British Austin Maxi for sale. It had a Gibraltar registration and number plates, so one evening I went on the local bus to see the car. I asked the bus driver when I should get off and, in Urbanization Richmar, I met John and Maureen Franks who owned the villa Casa Habana in Marbella and were selling their car. They needed somebody to look after their property while they were travelling to and from the UK, and so I moved into the property as a caretaker for them.

I cancelled my hostel reservation because it was out of my living budget. At the villa – between my caretaker duties of looking after a German shepherd called Brutus, whose bark was worse than his bite, and a lovely fun dog to take for walks on the beach – I travelled to Meknès and Fèz in Morocco, and to Faro in Portugal. On both trips I used the ferries to take my car to these countries and some wonderful experiences came out of my travelling and meeting people.

John and Maureen had a business contact in Florida who was looking to expand his wholesale travel agency. I was very interested in going to America to live and work, as in past years I had visited the US on a travel visa. I met up with John Betts of Bestours at a friend's house in London when I returned from Spain and my adventures. John was in London on a business trip, so he set up a time for us to meet. By June 1987 I was in Naples, Florida, working for Bestours as a travel consultant. Things didn't work out at the position that I had been offered, so, as I had a connection in Cardiff-by-the-Sea in California, I moved from the East Coast of the US to the West Coast on 1 August 1987. In one month I had got myself a job, a car and a place to live!

Back in 1985, when I visited the US on an educational exchange visit with Camp America, I worked at B'nai B'rith Perlman Camp for the summer with American children in Pennsylvania. This is how I obtained my first piece of identification – a valid social security card and number issued to me by the Department of Social Security. At that time, in the period before 9/11, documents were easier to obtain. I applied for the card and number at the American Legion in the small town of Hancock, New York, across the Delaware River from where I was working at the camp in Pennsylvania. In two weeks the card came and, unlike today, it did not have the usual stamp on it which says 'NOT VALID FOR WORK'.

At that time I had to return to the UK as my then visa was about to expire, but I knew I would be back in the US in the not-too-distant future. I arrived back in Florida first and then moved on to California on August 1st 1987. In a way, though, I looked at Pennsylvania as being my other place of birth – other than Wales, that is. Once in California I started life as I wanted to continue and applied for a Californian driver's licence, went for the driving test and passed, and was issued my Californian driver's licence by the Department of Motor Vehicles at Plaza Drive, Oceanside, California in 1987. To show proof of my date of birth I actually gave them my British birth certificate with my application. This, again, was before the tragic events of 9/11 when the whole world changed. A social security card and Californian driver's licence were all I needed to live the good life as a law-abiding resident.

America is indeed a wonderful country in which to live and work and there are a lot of opportunities. I worked at various positions; one was for a local cable TV company called Daniels Cablevision in Carlsbad for twelve years as a fleet technician. Mr Bill Daniels was a dear man and has been called the father of cable TV, as he came up with the concept. I also worked at Villa Encinitas in Encinitas where I lived. Villa Encinitas was an assisted living home for people with cancer and Alzheimer's.

Then I progressed to working at a world-renowned cancer research facility, the Burnham Institute in La Jolla, California. The research at the Burnham Institute covers stem cells, Alzheimer's, ageing and other areas of medicine. Some 500 scientists from all over the world work there. I worked there as a facilities mechanic. The job was a challenge every day, and I thoroughly enjoyed interacting with all the scientists and doctors while working on projects in the laboratories. There are some marvellous people there, dedicated to their research to find cures. I was indeed living the American dream!

In 2005 I applied for a US passport at the local post office in Encinitas where I was living. I was technically an illegal alien, as the US Immigration and Naturalization Service would term it, but I was getting older and had concerns for my future. I wanted to spend my retirement in the US, so I needed American documentation to show my date of birth. I had been a state and federal taxpayer for all the nineteen years that I had lived in the US as a resident. Under the very definition of the word in any dictionary, a citizen is an inhabitant of a city, which I had been – in the city of San Diego, with a clean driver's license. This all changed on December 2nd 2005 at 6.50 a.m. on a cold morning as I arrived to work at my usual time at the Burnham Institute.

The Arrest

It was the start of a usual working day, the last day of the work week – a Friday. I arrived at the Burnham Institute and started to back my Geo Metro into its usual parking space when I noticed a vehicle at the end of the parking lot. There seemed to be a red light on the dashboard in the centre of the windshield.

At the moment I noticed the vehicle, all hell broke loose. Diplomatic Security Service agents appeared from nowhere in vehicles and blocked my car in; with guns drawn and pointing at me, they surrounded me, shouting, 'Stay where you are! Put your hands on top of the car!'

I had no idea what was happening, but remained quite calm and complied with the instructions. I saw my safety officer walking across the street looking dumbfounded as to what was going on. He questioned the officers as to why I was being arrested; some of my other work colleagues also came up to see what was going on as I was being read my Miranda rights, handcuffed and placed in the back of an agent's car. I also questioned the agents as to why I was being arrested – with no reply.

I was searched and my car was searched for weapons. I still had no idea what was happening. I was asked if I had any guns in the car.

I said, 'No!' *Guns?* I thought. *What on earth is he talking about?*

At that point I decided that it was in my interests to remain silent. I was placed in the back of a cramped car (all the room was for the driver and passenger up front). I asked if they could move their seats forward, but as I was caged in with a metal barrier between me and the other occupants of the car, I had to manage. One of the officers told me to get as comfortable as I could. We headed off on Interstate 5 south towards San Diego, to the agents' office downtown. When we arrived, I was helped out of the car, as my hands were cuffed behind me, and an officer took a firm grip of the cuffs, just in case I was going to run off. Not that I had anywhere to run to! We all got into the elevator and went up to the second floor where I was fingerprinted and placed in a holding cell.

One officer produced the US passport application that I had sent in the year before.

'Isn't this you in the photograph?' he asked.

Numerous times I replied that I would prefer to remain silent, but I was still asked further questions – a clear violation of my Miranda rights. This is a common tactic that arresting officers use to coerce a confession from a suspect, with, of course, another agent present to witness any confession. Anybody arrested has the right to remain silent, and is innocent until proven guilty. None of this concerns the agents, who want to use the power that they have during an arrest. At one point one agent wanted to know why I had handed in the application. I declined to answer, saying that I preferred to remain silent until I saw legal council. He persisted, and then asked me a strange question: was I a terrorist? Did I have any connection to the IRA?

Again, he was violating my rights, as I had told him many times of my wish to remain silent. I did, under duress, answer the agent and said, 'No! I am not a terrorist!'

After a short time in the holding cell, I was then taken by car to the rear ramp entrance of Metropolitan Correctional Center (MCC) in San Diego, a holding prison. The agents handed me over to the booking officer. He checked my belongings, cash was recorded and I signed the receipt, then was given a copy. This was the first time that I had ever set foot in a prison in my life! The area was very cold, with concrete walls and floors, thick, black, four-inch-wide bars all the way to the high ceilings. The holding cells also had concrete walls, and each had a metal toilet and a concrete seating area. It was a frightening experience to see all this.

After passing through a metal detector, I was then told by the officer to go behind a cloth screen and take off all my clothes.

Naked as the day that I was born, I was asked to hold my arms up high, turn around, squat and cough! Then I was issued white socks, a white T-shirt, boxers (I hate boxers!), a white jumpsuit and a pair of comfortable blue canvas shoes made in China.

When I had dressed, a female Filipino nurse arrived and started to take my medical information. She asked first if I was thinking of committing suicide.

I replied, 'No, madam!' A lot of thoughts *were* going through my mind though. What was my future now? I had a lot more to live for; I didn't want to throw my life away. I was scared, tired and fearful of the unknown, but still remained as calm as I could. After answering the lady, I was taken to Floor D housing unit. This floor is similar to G-7, where I was eventually going to spend my time on a general population floor. Floor D housing unit is for new arrivals and usually, when there is room on the general population floors, inmates are moved out of it as soon as possible, within a few days. Inside each cell is a metal toilet with no seat, a metal handbasin with cold water, and two bunk beds, each with a dirty old, torn mattress. I first thought that the funding for prisons must have gone down over the years, as it was like a third world prison cell; but all this turned out to be for the shock effect to an inmate of coming into prison. I must admit that it did shock me.

My cell looked out on to the buildings of downtown San Diego. We were locked up in this cell for six hours a day, and let out for breakfast, lunch and dinner and to use the bathroom at those times. Then we were locked up for the night. My cellmate was Ronaldo, a Mexican national from Tijuana who had lived in Los Angeles with his family for twenty-two years.

He had been caught crossing back over the border into the US, having gone to attend to family matters in Mexico. I can relate to this; I did the same in 2003 when I returned to the United Kingdom to see a family member who was getting on in age and was ill. In 2005, prior to my arrest in December, the family member I visited did actually pass on, so I was glad that I was able to spend some time with him before that happened. It is unfortunate when one has to take risks in life to be with family, especially if part of the family live in a country other than the one in which you decide to live.

I did not sleep for the first few nights in prison, which is quite common for new inmates. In fact, I did not sleep at all for the next two and a half weeks and was quite interested to see how this would affect me mentally. Would I lose it in this new environment? What else was in store for me? My questions were soon to be answered.

It helped me to look at the lights of the north side of the downtown buildings, and to pray to God to give me the strength to continue. I also prayed for my cellmate, Ronaldo, who seemed a gentle, decent person who didn't deserve to be in this type of situation at his time in life. He was in his late fifties.

The cell had drab, dirty white walls and a white, popcorn-textured ceiling; there was constant noise from the floors above from toilets that seemed to be flushing twenty-four hours a day. Did the other inmates up above never sleep either? Any person who experiences all this first-hand feels a sense of hopelessness and fears that life could well be over. The Correctional Officer (CO), I later found out, liked to run the floor a certain way, treating new arrivals with military discipline. He liked to shout a lot, and it was like having a staff sergeant bark orders all the time.

The Terrorist Theory

When I was arrested, as I have said, the Diplomatic Security Service (DSS) agent asked me if I was a terrorist and if I had any connections with the IRA. I had wanted to laugh at these questions – they were so ridiculous! But I responded to the question with a firm, 'No, I am not a terrorist.' The agent had continued with some more follow-up questions, even though I had exercised my right to remain silent. So I had done just that, and had refused to answer any more of his ludicrous questions.

He had wanted to know why I had applied for a US passport at all, as I already had a British passport that was valid. I had nothing to hide, but I wasn't going to give him the rope that he could hang me with before I had even got to a court of law. I just said time and time again that I preferred to remain silent, and the questions did eventually stop.

It seemed that the US government still wanted to pursue this terrorist theory when I was at MCC. I had a strange experience one day. I got called into the CO's office on inspection day. I went there to sign for some legal mail from the counsellor. It appeared that the ATF (the Bureau of Alcohol, Tobacco and Firearms), along with the FBI, were looking into my background during my time in the US. They wouldn't find anything out of the ordinary, as there wasn't anything to find, except that I had lived (as far as I was concerned) an exemplary life in the US until the day of my arrest.

The CO on duty that day asked me, 'Why are the ATF looking into your background, Jones?'

It was partly out of curiosity that he asked the question, as he knew me to be a very unassuming person, always polite when I had any contact with him.

'I have no idea, sir,' I replied.

He then added that he had no problem with me.

'I have no problem with you, either, sir,' I said. To this day I

The brochure for the gun range I visited in 2005
Thank you, Marc

have no idea why he said that he 'had no problem' with me. Maybe he though that I did have terrorist connections.

I could only recall one time, about six month previously, that I had been in a gun range during my entire nineteen years of living in the US, but just this one visit set the US government departments on a wild goose chase to try and find something that wasn't there to find. They feared that I might have a connection with a terrorist group. Perhaps the fact that I didn't even have a parking ticket in all the years that I had lived in San Diego had aroused some suspicion.

The one time I had visited a gun range had been on a Saturday afternoon in San Diego when I was driving past it. I had thought that, as I had never been in a gun range or shot a gun, I should stop by, as I wanted to see what went on. At this particular range, I found out that you would have had to go on to the range with a member and pay a fee to use the range to shoot the member's gun, which was registered to that owner. So, not knowing a person with a registered gun or a member of that range, I was out of luck that day and left the range after observing a few people shooting their weapons. Because of this one visit I was investigated by the ATF and the FBI. The US government were fishing so hard to find something on me, but like all fishermen will tell you, sometimes it is a waste of time as there isn't anything to catch!

Prison Life at Metropolitan Correctional Center (MCC)

When we were eventually moved up to G-7, the general population floor, myself and another nine inmates in our white jumpsuits were welcomed with a loud roar as incoming new kids on the block!

There are over 1,000 inmates at MCC. All the other inmates were wearing their military green jumpsuits. Different jumpsuit colours signify the various reasons for incarceration. An inmate wearing an orange suit is a 'snitch'; a blue suit is from another correctional centre; a red suit is an inmate who is charged with a more serious crime and is violent at times, and so on. All the inmates were very friendly as we came on to the floor. 97% of the inmates on this floor were Hispanic; MCC is sometimes called the 'Mexican Country Club'. I remember my first encounter with Alberto. He spoke very good English and welcomed me straight away to G-7. I had also started to establish a friendship with Julio, who was on D with me, and I trusted Julio somewhat (that is, as far as you can really trust anybody in prison). Julio said I should be careful, as everybody seemed to be too friendly – this is something that all new arrivals to a prison have to be wary of. Our new home on G-7 was very noisy; guys played card games, dominoes and generally seemed to be having a great time. There was a lot of laughter and the atmosphere was very upbeat.

The CO on the floor showed us where our bunks were. I had the top bunk in a small alcove; there was a window that looked east towards Horton Plaza, a shopping mall in downtown San Diego, and, beyond that, towards the mountains of Mexico in the far distance. I was issued two clean bed sheets and two blankets, a pillowcase, and there was already a pillow on the bed. I was quite lucky, as pillows were hard to come by and I didn't have a pillow on Floor D so I had a lot of neck pains, partly due to all the stress. Studies have shown that a person cannot last very long without sleep. This is completely wrong in my case and, as I have said, I was quite interested in finding out the result of how lack of sleep would affect me mentally.

I was issued my new clothes: two new military green jump-suits, new boxers, new T-shirts and new socks. I also received a toiletry bag containing toothpaste, a toothbrush, and some small bars of soap; and I was given two hand towels, a comb and a plastic razor. After making my bed I was met by another inmate called Malcolm, who introduced me to Smith. Malcolm gave me a tour of MCC. He was about twenty-seven, 6 ft 2 and in good shape. Originally from Texas, Malcolm was a student in San Diego. Smith, an older gentleman in his late fifties, who wore glasses with a broken, taped-up side, was from Alaska. When on the outside, he worked on the fishing boats; he had served some time in the military in Cambodia and Vietnam, had married once, and was inside for conspiracy. Malcolm was inside for drug manufacture in college.

As Malcolm showed me around, he started to tell me about all the procedures. The councillor at that time was an African-American man. He was due to leave in a few weeks, but Malcolm explained that he liked to see all beds made by 7.30 a.m. every morning, 'and don't piss him off if you want him to do anything for you!' Malcolm added. We went into the common bathroom area, which consisted of two toilets with plastic seats separated by metal partitions. There were no doors to the cubicles. Malcolm said that one was the 'pisser' and one was the 'shitter', the reason being that guys tended to pee on the seat, so they tried to keep one sanitary for that reason. There was also a strong smell of urine and five handbasins in the bathroom.

This was my new home in Range 5, on G-7. Prison life con-sists of routine every day of the week, and all the days blend into one day that is the same. You get up at the same time every morning and go to bed at the same time every evening; you eat at the same time every day and you have count (that is, are counted) at the same times every day. Laundry for whites is collected on the same day every week and coloured items are also collected on the same day each week.

There are set days and times on which you can go to the law

library after a form called a 'cop out' has been put in the internal mailbox to the library CO. He then looks at your request and places your 'register number' – an inmate's ID – on the call-out list. After an inmate's name is on the call-out list, which is posted daily on a bulletin board, the inmate can go to the law library at the set times noted. There are also call-outs for medical exams, and the floor CO on duty usually calls out the last name of the inmate who has to go to a medical. Some COs want to know at breakfast at 6 a.m. if you have a request to go to the law library so they can pull an inmate's photo ID card and have it ready to pass on to the elevator CO who will take you there (all inmates have to be accounted for when going off a general population floor to another area of the holding prison). The same process takes place when inmates are back on the general population floor: photo ID cards are handed back to account for the inmates being present back on the floor, and back in their range for count time.

Altogether there are eight ranges on G-7. Range 1 is up above, Range 2 below, Range 3 above and Range 4 below. Range 5, where I was, was above, 6 below, 7 above and 8 below. There were a total of thirty-seven inmates in Ranges 5 and 6 who all shared the one bathroom in Range 5. We also only had one shower for us all to use. The hand rail along the wall down to the shower door was used to tie our small hand towels in order of who was to shower next. The person coming out of the shower would shout 'Shower!' to signify it was free for the next person in case they were away somewhere else playing cards. If he didn't show in a minute or two, the next person in line would go in. All hand towels were tied in a way that the person knew it was their towel, and their turn. Some would put initials in pen on the towel. This system worked quite well.

Some of the guys would play around and would flick the shower light switch off and on when a person was inside. On one occasion I saw Smith come out of the shower, soaking wet, with his boxer shorts on, to reprimand the inmate who had turned off the light while he was showering. Smith's sight was failing, so if he lost his soap and it was dark he could easily have slipped. That is why he was so angry at the person who shut the light off. On another occasion a different inmate was in the shower and the guys threw a container of ice through the top bars of the door. He just took it in his stride, as the guys were always fooling around. In some ways the inmates acted like kids at camp, and MCC lived up to its 'Mexican Country Club' nickname.

In the common area, between the ranges, were metal stools which were secured to metal tables; this area seated forty-eight inmates. Here, we would have breakfast, lunch and dinner, one range at a time. One day, we ate all meals before 1.30 p.m., on a very disorganised Super Bowl Sunday (2005). It was organised by a supposed veteran CO of fifteen years' service who knew how to run a floor – yeah, right! He just wanted to go early to watch the game!

The seating was in a 'U' shape. There was a clear area in the middle where a pool table used to sit. Prior to my arrival, members of two local gangs – the 'Southsiders' and 'Pisces' – were placed on this same floor. When I found out about this I could never for the life of me understand the logic of a prison system that would place members of two gangs on the same floor with a pool table – a pool table with cues and hard pool balls! The end result of this was, of course, a fight over some disagreement; both gangs used the cues as weapons, and placed the balls in net laundry bags, swinging them as gladiators would in the arena. A riot squad eventually put a stop to all the bloodshed. Two inmates, so I later learned, were carried off unconscious with bloodied heads and skull fractures. To this day there is an indent in the tiled floor of G-7 where one swinging weapon (fortunately) missed its victim but did considerable damage to the concrete. Those that started the riot are looking at an additional fifteen to twenty years for attempted murder.

During my time on this floor, I must admit that, thankfully, I never saw any violence of this magnitude. Still, I was in prison, where anything can and does happen. When new inmates first arrive, they are usually very upset at leaving their family and friends to come into this new environment. Many cry at night, are frustrated and anxious. You can always tell a new inmate from their constant bounding right knee or continual tapping of the feet; this can also signify boredom. Every day an inmate must work out what to do with the hours of each new 'Groundhog Day': play cards, watch TV, exercise, read books... One thing that you learn while being incarcerated is to numb your feelings. It does take some time to get over this prison experience in life. You are also afraid of an uncertain future: what might happen once you have served your sentence and are released? You also take nothing for granted; since you have no expectations of life, you welcome whatever good things happen. You even wonder if you will ever be able to acknowledge any feelings again in life – to love, feel sad, happy – and go on in life. This, of course, will all come one day and life will be happier and a lot better than this prison existence. Every step you take will be for a better future eventually.

All inmates had their routines. Some watched TV, either all day or at certain times. Others worked out on the stationary exercise bike or ran up and down the stairs from the top range to the bottom range. We had an exercise bike in Range 5 and there was another bike in Range 1. Inmates from any range could use the bikes on a first-come basis. Some inmates used to use the exercise bike to lift up as a bar bell to build up their arm muscles and release the daily frustration of being incarcerated. Inmates are very resourceful; Malcolm used to fill two plastic bags with water, wrap both separately in spare sheets, then place them in two net laundry bags and hang the bags over each end of a broom handle removed from the brush part. This would be used by all the guys as a bar bell for exercise when the gym of Range 5 was open.

A large brown bin was placed in the front of the toilet in Range 5 for some sort of privacy when people were on the toilet. The water bags would be placed in the bin for storage when they were not in use. One of the COs would take great pleasure in moving the bin out of the bathroom from in front of the toilet, sometimes saying that there was 'no privacy afforded here'. He would shake the bin to see if weight was in the bottom (i.e. the water bags) and would then announce that if he found out who had put the bags in the bin, he would place the bags on that inmate's bed and burst them. He liked to run G-7 as he would run D floor: with military discipline. Some guys said he was a wannabe Marine, though he had never actually been in the Corps.

In prison a person sometimes comes alive, mentally, with the stimulation of everything that goes on every day and the constant noise. I used to joke with Malcolm and we both would shout above all noise to say, 'We love noise! Noise is good!' Of course, we were jesting. It is indeed another world in prison, a world of its own. And although some people become more alive in prison, using all their mental ability, and learning to survive in this new environment, some inmates go the opposite way. Some inmates will not think for themselves; they zone out, watch too much TV and tune out. Then others help them, and they become too dependant on this help. If they are in the prison system for a long period, this is the worst thing that could be done for them as they don't learn how to survive. So there is a balance of helping, but not too much; the inmate must also help themselves. I suppose the analogy is like being out in the wilderness: you either learn to survive or you simply die. After all, this is a tough environment and watching too much TV in prison numbs the senses, so you don't use all your mental capacity. MCC is a holding prison, and I can understand why guys worked out so much to build up muscle and strength and get into peak fitness, in case they had problems in the future when they started to serve their sentences in tougher prisons.

I felt in some ways that God had placed me in this situation for a reason and so I looked for ways of how I could make the most of my time in prison.

I contacted the Cardiff-by-the-Sea Library which I was a member of and had been going to for a number of years. My request to the library was from one inmate in a government institution to another government agency: could the Cardiff library supply MCC with old worn-out books that were of no use to the library? I knew that the library often tried to sell off such books at weekend book sales, and that not many people bought them. I had a very nice postcard from the librarian saying that he would go through the proper government channels and see what could be done.

Upon one visit to the law library in the following weeks, I saw a pile of old books that had just arrived. So that brought a smile to my face and inspired me to write to another library in

Rancho Santa Fe with the same request. I had also frequented this library on many a Saturday afternoon. I modelled myself in some ways on the Tim Robbins character in the film *The Shawshank Redemption*, when he wrote letters requesting books and started a library in prison. Does art imitate life or does life imitate art?

Meeting Malcolm was a big help to me, and I am still in contact with him by letter. He helped me in many ways to get through a tough period of my life, for which I am eternally grateful. He loaned me a spare radio that he had, with earphones with which I could try to tune out the daily noise of the general population floor. I also made use of my time to help other inmates set up their own 'power of attorney' (POA), as Malcolm had showed me how to set up mine. One inmate wanted his wife to have the power to sell his cars, as he was the registered owner. Another wanted his mother as POA so she could have custody of his child while he was inside, and the child would not be put into care. Another just wanted me to go over a statement that he was going to make in court, so I was very happy to be able to help all these guys as best as I could. There was a lot of support inside; we all helped each other, without ulterior motive, other than it was good to help each other. I also immersed myself in writing every day as there was so much to write about.

At first some of the guys who came near my bed were suspicious of me, and in the small space of a corner there wasn't too much that we all didn't know about each other and our daily routines. Some thought that I was writing a report about everybody, which I was, in some ways, of my daily observations, but not in any way about the cases of the various guys that were around me. So in time they knew that, and a sort of trust was established. I actually showed one of the guys, who had the nickname 'Splinter', what I was writing one day; he took all the pages as I was sat on my top bunk bed. His eyes glanced at the words, moving from side to side, with me knowing full well that he was very limited in reading English, just as I was in reading Spanish. I just laughed, and so did he.

The guys bunking near me were involved in a large drug conspiracy case, so often eight to ten of them would gather to discuss aspects of their case after seeing their attorney. The conversation was in Spanish, so I was unaware of what was said.

It was obvious to me that one person was the head person of the case; he also happened to be the number-one person on G-7, at the head of the 'chain of command'. He controlled all the eight ranges and 210 inmates on the general population floor.

Inspection Day and Roof Recreation

After breakfast on a Wednesday mornings the floor unit supervisor would come around to inspect. This day was also a chance for the supervisor to bring guests along to ensure the inmates were properly cared for and all ranges were looking their best, like a well-run military barracks. The CO on duty would bellow high-pitched orders over the noise of the floor-polishing machines which inmates operated in their ranges. Two machines worked their way through all eight ranges.

The one shower serving Ranges 5 and 6 would be cleaned from top to bottom, walls scrubbed clean, and the two toilets disinfected. Range 5 contained five handbasins for the thirty-seven inmates of both Range 5 and Range 6 to share. We managed quite well.

Sometimes, on a Wednesday, I stayed back from going to the recreation area on the roof, when most inmates would be herded up while inspection was conveniently carried out with very few inmates on the general population floor. Overcrowding on the prison floor didn't seem to exist at such times. It was nice to stay back on occasion and enjoy the peace and quiet, as at other times the noise level was very high, day and night.

At night, all the snorers took over in their deep slumber, unaware of how everybody else was awake. We did ask a floor counsellor if all the snorers could be kept in one area away from all the other ranges. That request was met with a notice on the window in the counsellor's office: 'NO BED CHANGES'. So we all managed as best we could. I made some earplugs out of a few sheets of toilet paper and a piece of cling film off Malcolm's special diet tray that he had daily (he had decided to become Buddhist and so his tray didn't include any meat, just soya products). I would cover my little finger with the sheets of toilet paper like a glove, then place the cling film over the paper, twist off the end, and place in the ear canal to fit. Pushed in a bit, it sealed the ear, and kept out a lot of the constant daily and night noise. It helped me to get a few hours' sleep, before a new Groundhog Day began again.

All beds were made neatly by 7.30 a.m. each morning; for the most part all ranges carried out this practice – there were very few unmade beds. We all cooperated with the CO on duty; this helped him to look good for the unit supervisor. One particular CO operated on the basis of 'you scratch my back, and I'll scratch yours'. We would help him in having well-run, clean ranges on G-7, and he would, in turn, comply with our daily requests for pencils, writing paper, envelopes, small bars of soap and toilet paper, which he handed out when in stock; supplies went very quickly. Every time we wanted a new toilet roll, we would have to take back the old cardboard roll to prove it had been used. It was the same with razors, which had plastic blades but were quite sharp, and could be used once or twice before being discarded in the CO's office trash bin.

This is how the trade-off system worked. As MCC was a holding prison, the conditions were exceptionally good for the federal prison system, compared to lower operating budgets for state-run prisons. Some inmates that I spoke to informed me that state prisons were a lot worse.

On a Wednesday we would all collect on the roof to pick up any commissary purchases. We each had a number and would line up with our net laundry bags to fill them with items like Cup a Soups, candy, potato chips, lotion or shampoo products, packet razors better than the ones we usually had issued, and packets of tuna (a favourite with the guys who make snacks before going to bed). Some guys bought training shoes or small radios with earphones; word soon passed on that any items like those had to be left behind when the inmate was released. So inmates just passed down these items, even though the inmates paid for these products out of their own commissary accounts. It's another way the federal prisons make money. There is no limit to how much money an inmate can hold in his account, but there was a limit on how much could be spent every week: up to $290.

Some inmates worked in the kitchens or as laundry workers for 60c a day. A fellow inmate, Smith, had worked for just over a year as a kitchen worker, so his salary was raised to 90c a day, and he worked six days a week. He said he liked going to work at 5 a.m.; he could eat what he liked and the money came in handy for buying a few commissary items, mainly batteries for his radio, with his budget of $21.60 a month. He had no family to support him while he was inside, and he longed to return to the fishing boats of Alaska. I'm sure he will one day, when he is released.

We also went to the roof for recreation; there was a handball court, a volleyball net and a basketball hoop. Some guys walked or pace walked, some sat in the sun and talked with fellow inmates, one or two might karate kick or punch the padded pillars around the walk area (partly, I suspect, out of frustration, or a sign to other inmates not to mess with them). Any violence on the general population floor would result in a trip to the 'hole' for both inmates, so this was a deterrent, in part. I saw very little violence, thankfully, on G-7, and problems between inmates were taken care of with punishment handed out quickly and situations resolved by the 'chain of command'. I did once witness such an incident, when one inmate stole an item from another's locker. The offender said he had permission to take the item, so both parties were brought together, the situation discussed and the truth finally came out. A quick blow to the offender sorted things out, the item was returned, and that was that.

We had Bible study every Monday and Thursday with Brother Stefan, an inmate. He taught the Bible in English and Spanish and was a godsend to many at MCC. His case was complicated, involving drugs and conspiracy, and he had been at MCC for three years. He brought a lot of hope to everybody who attended, and we also had a prayer meeting on Saturday evenings with Stefan. One Sunday morning at sunrise it was a wonderful sight to see the bright red and orange streaks across the sky over the distant mountain ranges of Mexico. My bunk bed was by a barred window that faced east over downtown San Diego. I felt a sadness for all the lost souls that were at MCC but gave thanks at Mass that morning and prayed for them.

Some new arrivals would cry at Bible study when they first came, sad for what they had done, and I think they cried for their families left behind. Million-dollar views of San Diego Bay for million-dollar inmates incarcerated. The Convention Center lay to the south, as did the Coronado Bay Bridge; to the west was the harbour, boats sailing by every day. The spirit on G-7 was very uplifting. There was laughter every day, and lots of noise, except between 10 p.m. and 6 a.m. – which was officially quiet time – when the snorers took over instead. Inmates' anxiety was constant. Stress rashes on arms were common, due to the living conditions. Baby powder would clear up this type of rash, or hydrocortisone cream, which could be purchased at commissary. Weight loss was also common, as well as weight gain. This all depended on the metabolism of the inmate, the regular prison diet and exercise, and how each individual person's body reacted to all the stress. A person can also age very quickly under such conditions: grey hairs appeared daily and some inmates' facial features changed relatively quickly, becoming old, worn faces in just a few months.

In Corinthians 15:51 and Philippians 3:21 God is working to change us in Christ-like ways. I believe that this has been shown to me in many ways throughout my life as joy, peace, patience, love, kindness, faithfulness and self-control, as in Galatians 5:22–5:23. I'm not perfect in every way, but have changed and started to find a lot of inner joy, maybe not expressed, but it has always been there. Faithfulness and kindness have always been with me; I believe I should always do unto others as I would have them do unto me.

I hope for the best in life, because it's the best you can hope for. It is so easy to just give up, throw in the towel as we say in the UK for whatever situation you encounter in life, and then be angry at yourself for giving up so easily and not fighting. I am pleased at how I conducted myself in prison: I sometimes questioned authority in a non-confrontational way, but I was humble and obeyed the rules in a daily controlled environment. I kept my self-respect and also respected others, COs and fellow inmates alike, at both facilities, MCC and CCA, and forged relationships that might or might not endure the test of time after my release. Some inmates insist that they have no friends inside and don't trust anybody; it is also a challenge to trust anybody on the outside when released.

The guys in my range were very creative. One morning before lunch, Alonzo had cut strips of paper about 5 cm wide by 25 cm long and used it as a template to cut chip packets (crisp packets) into strips. He would wash the foil interior clean and cut the packet up using a plastic blade taken out of a disposable razor (these blades were very sharp and were also used to sharpen pencils). The strips were then folded and weaved into a red and silver frame, the photo of a family member slid in between the frame, and a piece of yarn used to hang the frame under the top bunk and over the person who owned it as a reminder of hope for what futures they still had to live for.

One of the frames made from crisp packets by an inmate

The guys also drew from books and magazines, decorated envelopes of letters sent to family members, and made crucifixes from yarn.

On Saturday one of the COs was up to his old tricks, walking around taking clothes off the pipes that were hand washed and hanging out to dry by the air vents. Some guys liked to wash their items of issued clothing by hand, like T-shirts and boxers, as the laundry service sometimes wasn't very good. But regulations quoted that nothing should be hanging off the pipes above, which were for the sprinkler system in case of a fire. It was a cat-and-mouse game; COs tried to snatch the clothing before we noticed them coming. I managed to beat the CO to my sweater that was drying, a sweater that I had purchased from commissary. He beat me to the sweater later when I put it back up a second time and I didn't get to it first. I said nothing, of course, and just let it go. He could keep it! He would confiscate clothing from all ranges as part of his government job and showed very little compassion to the inmates that he disliked.

Once I requested a sick call appointment. The appointment was for the following month so I sent back the little part of the form at the bottom and said that I would probably be dead from the flu symptoms that I had, so I cancelled the appointment. Two days later I was called to the medical floor for an exam and given Ibuprofen, but most of my symptoms had gone by then. Dental exams were non-existent inside, and one inmate had to get a court order to have a rotten tooth extracted. No mouthwash could be purchased at commissary, at it is alcohol-based, so we made do with a salt-water mouthwash and purchased toothpaste at commissary. Some inmates had friends smuggle in dental floss at visiting times. The floss would be handed over when holding hands with a family member or girlfriend and smuggled back to the range.

On shake down day, one by one, all ranges would line up in the common area. Some guys would rush back to their lockers to rip up pieces of paper then flush them down the toilet, just in case the notes could get them into some sort of trouble. We were all patted down by hand first, then had a metal detector waved up and down to detect any self-made weapons. Then we all filed out to go to the roof while CO personnel searched bedding and lockers for any contraband. Smith had a spare jumpsuit taken – that really pissed him off! Because he worked in the kitchen, he needed an extra jumpsuit due to all the food being splashed on him while working. He eventually put in for another jumpsuit via a clothing request.

I always used to leave a pamphlet from the British Consul in my locker, so I never had everything turned upside down too much. Not that there was anything to find in the locker, other than toiletry items, books, etc.

From MCC Law Library

Ten Commandments: Full Moon Prayer

1. Treat the earth and all that dwell there with respect.
2. Remain close to the great spirit.
3. Show great respect for your fellow beings.
4. Work together for the benefit of all mankind (give assistance and kindness wherever needed).
5. Do what you know to be right.
6. Look after the well-being of mind and body.
7. Dedicate a share of your efforts to the greater good.
8. Be truthful and honest at all times.
9. Take full responsibility for your actions.
10. Do unto others as you would have them do unto you.

Mitakuye Oyasin

Chain of Command

There was always a lot of activity near my bunk bed since it was situated right next to the lockers. Guys would go back and forth to the locker daily, taking items out, mainly food. It was evident that this was more than just a person's store locker, and I soon deduced that this was a second storage locker for one of the inmates.

We were issued only one locker by MCC for personal items so I did wonder how he happened to have two. He was the number-one person on the general population floor and had control over all the eight ranges on that floor in such a quiet way that even some of the inmates on the floor didn't know. He had a very high balance in his commissary account; outside sources in Mexico would pay into it. These funds would be used to buy protection and any muscle that he might need, by ways of paying another inmate to be the tough guy to sort out any problems – in a non-violent way, I might add, just in very persuasive arm-twisting ways.

For this help, the bouncer or other hired help could pick and choose any food items from the locker, and also be helped in other ways, such as having a new pair of training shoes or a new radio purchased from commissary on the roof. Other items hard to come by, like stamps, envelopes, paper or pens, would also be in the locker (along with batteries for the radios) for inmates to help themselves to at any times.

Other guys were also on the payroll in this way, like kitchen and laundry workers who would supply Number One with extra food from the kitchens, or extra items of clothing if needed. Guys were also paid to clean Range 5 shower where I was; they would clean from top to bottom every day, and other ranges were also cleaned. The standards of hygiene were high. Other guys were paid in this way to be the ears in all the ranges and report what was going on, and there wasn't much that Number One didn't know about, all the time, of what went on in all the ranges.

I didn't envy the task that he must have had to keep up with all that did go on, as he was also still working on his very complicated case at the same time. So, in my estimation, he had his hands full; but he seemed to enjoy having all this business to attend to every day.

Inmates on the payroll were paid a lot more than if an inmate decided to get a work position at MCC, where, as I mentioned, he would be paid 60c a day to work nine hours in the kitchen or as a laundry worker. On the other hand, a bouncer for Number One would be paid $10 a week or more for his services.

Guys cleaning the shower would also be first in line to use it, which was fair. The high standards of hygiene benefited all ranges, but our range was by far the cleanest. I suggested to Number One that he give the guys a break cleaning, and that we all should take it in turns to clean the range every day and to clean the bathroom and shower. He mentioned to me that they were paid to do the cleaning, but still saw my point of view. So we then started a rota for every guy in Ranges 5 and 6 to take a turn to clean. This system worked really well, and even Number One took his turn to mop the floors like the rest of us. This gave him even more credibility, and he was well liked anyhow.

In time, I established a respectful relationship with Number One; he would come to me to ask for advice on some subjects. He showed me pictures of his wife in Mexico and of his two lovely children, a little boy and a girl that he hoped to see again when released. His bail was set at $600,000 and he hoped to put his house up for the bail amount. I understood that his case was drug-related and that a number of guys were inside with him who were also involved in the case. I never asked too many questions as it wasn't my business, and the less that I knew the better.

I was concentrating on my own case and, more importantly, working on wrapping up my US life while I was at MCC as I knew that deportation was my inevitable fate at some time in the future, having had some spiritual guidance. I also tried to find out as much as I could about Correctional Corporations of America, or CCA, to see if I would be able to do anything while I would be there, as I knew I would be moved there soon. Guys told me that the phone calls were very expensive, $4 for the first minute, and $2 every other minute. They also told me about the food, and other things that went on at CCA, so my view was that I had to do all that I could while I was at MCC. When I saw my federal defender, I asked him to apply to the court for continuances, as I needed more time to wrap up my US life as far as I could. The courts were glad to oblige, as they would make more money off me the longer that they could keep me.

A lot of the guys were from very poor backgrounds in Tijuana, which is just across the border from San Diego. Some would hoard food in their stuffed lockers, extra food that was left over after breakfast, like cake or fruit. They would always share anything they had, especially at night-time after dinner and before quiet time when they would all congregate at the alcove where I was, mixing up a night-time snack of extra tuna, which they had somehow got from the kitchen, with some rice and vegetables. I would supply Doritos tortilla chips (crisps) for the dip, which I would purchase from commissary every week for them. The Hispanic people in general are very friendly, gregarious and family-orientated. I didn't understand all the Spanish, but could still get the gist of what they were talking about in their native tongue. They would laugh out loud and joke about everything until lights out. You would never think that we were all in a holding prison! I was asked to join them on a number of occasions, and I appreciated the invite to sample the snacks that they had prepared.

By chance, when in the law library one day, I also met Number Two. He was hard at work on the typewriter, and seemed to be helping a lot of guys, so I introduced myself and started to ask him some questions. At one time he had been the head of the chain of command, but gave up the position to be Number Two so he could concentrate more on his case. He was also Hispanic, and well versed in immigration law so he pointed me in the direction of various US laws that I wanted to research. We also established a good relationship while meeting once or twice a week at the law library. He helped me and many other inmates litigate our cases, asking for nothing in return.

There was not much that these two guys didn't know about

Zero Plus Dialing, Inc.

Important Information

This portion of your bill is provided as a service to the company identified above. Please review all charges appearing in this section. If you have any questions or concerns, call the telephone number shown above.

Current Charges

Long Distance

Vn	Date	Time	Place Called	Number	Code	Min	
Billed on Behalf of CUSTOM TELECONNECT							
Questions? Call: 1 800 228-0717							
Itemized Calls							
1.	2-14	4:35P	SAN DIEGO CA	819 235-1701	DB	3.0	13.16
2.	2-14	4:40P	SAN DIEGO CA	819 235-1709	DB	3.0	13.16
3.	2-14	4:54P	SAN DIEGO CA	819 235-1709	DB	3.0	13.16
Total Itemized Calls							39.48
Total CUSTOM TELECONNECT							39.48
Total Long Distance							39.48

Surcharges and Other Fees

4. State Regulatory Fee	.04

Government Fees and Taxes

5. CA High Cost Fund Surcharge - A.	.06
6. CA High Cost Fund Surcharge - B.	.79
7. California Teleconnect Fund Surcharge	.05
8. Universal Lifeline Telephone Service Surcharge	.51
9. CA Relay Service and Communications Devices Fund	.11
10. 9-1-1 Emergency System	.27
11. Federal	1.28
Total Government Fees and Taxes	3.04

Key to Calling Codes

B Collect	D Day

Total Zero Plus Dialing   42.56

Appoy: 12 calls
6 13.16 each
157.92
+ TAXS
12.16
$170.08

$4 A MIN
PHONE CALLS,
AT C.C.A!
TO A FRIEND TOM.

My phone bill at CCA
(phone calls for appointments at the US embassy in London are
£1.20 per minute.)

the goings on at MCC on the general population floors. They had eyes and ears everywhere to report back to them about anything that they needed to know. When some inmates got to know some information, one might shout out, 'Where is John Gotty?' if we had a meeting and Number One wasn't there. (Gotty was an American mobster convicted of his crimes who served time inside.) This chain of command was also instrumental in keeping the peace on all the general population floors, as there was still a mixture of San Diego Pisces and Southsiders on G-7.

I got to know quite a few of the guys, and we would have discussions every day on different topics. I found them to be very intelligent, streetwise guys. Some had no families, hence the gang had become their family. They also had very colourful personalities, and were very opinionated on what they believed in. Number One. I suppose that he might have come into prison from one of the drug cartels in Mexico, where he was used to having control, or he lacked the control on the outside which is why he was in prison in the first place! Inside, he could live in this controlled environment, but also have some sort of control that he didn't have on the outside.

Your Rights during Trial and Detention

If you have been arrested or detained, you do not lose your entitlement to your human rights. There are various international human rights treaties that contain provisions specific to trials and detention.

Individuals are entitled to a fair and public hearing within a reasonable time, and some treaties specify that a person is considered innocent until proven guilty beyond a reasonable doubt. A person can also be provided with an interpreter without charge in asylum cases. I found this out at CCA when I sat through fifteen cases until my case was heard there. Many international human rights treaties also prohibit torture and inhumane treatment or punishment and require that people in detention are treated with humanity.

If you ever feel threatened on a general population floor, when returning from court appearances you can also request not to be returned to that floor. It is important to obtain proper legal advice from a lawyer in respect of your rights in the country in which you are detained.

When you are read your Miranda rights in the US they state that you have the right to remain silent. You should exercise that right until you are appointed legal counsel. If you cannot afford an attorney, one will be appointed for you and your case from the federal defenders, or 'federal pretenders', as inmates call their attorneys. If you are not happy with the way your public defender is handling your case, you can fire your attorney and a new public defender will be appointed for you. The trial attorney that I had was very good with my case, but I did make the mistake of handing him, in confidence, pages one to sixteen of the start of this book in manuscript form. I said that he could read it, but requested that he then hand over the manuscript to my power of attorney to hold for me. He decided not to hand over the documents, as he noted in a letter to my power of attorney.

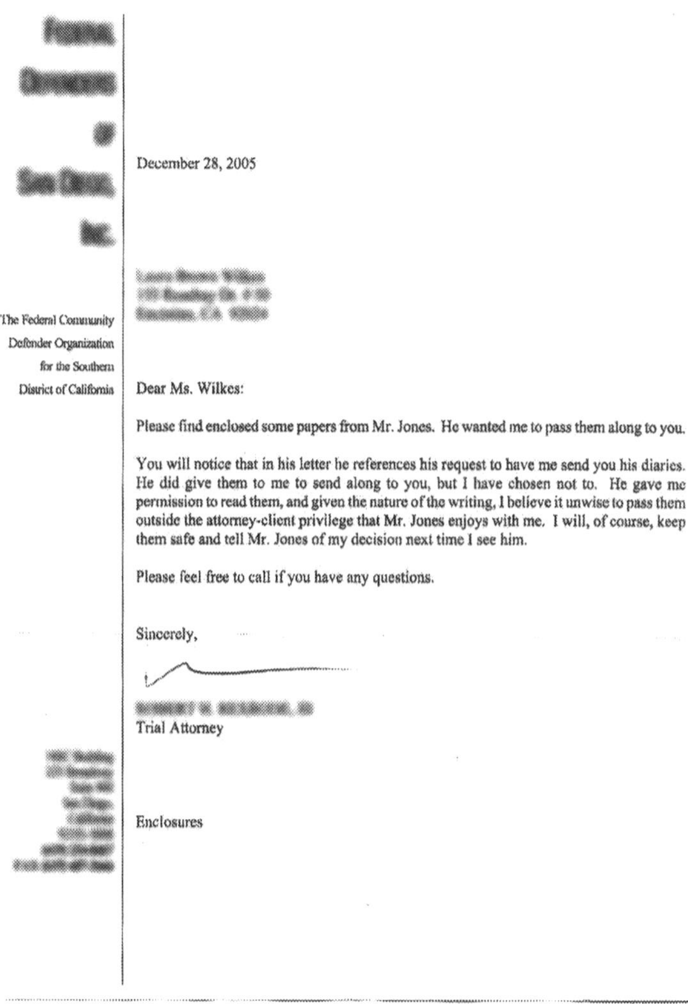

December 28, 2005

The Federal Community
Defender Organization
for the Southern
District of California

Dear Ms. Wilkes:

Please find enclosed some papers from Mr. Jones. He wanted me to pass them along to you.

You will notice that in his letter he references his request to have me send you his diaries. He did give them to me to send along to you, but I have chosen not to. He gave me permission to read them, and given the nature of the writing, I believe it unwise to pass them outside the attorney-client privilege that Mr. Jones enjoys with me. I will, of course, keep them safe and tell Mr. Jones of my decision next time I see him.

Please feel free to call if you have any questions.

Sincerely,

Trial Attorney

Enclosures

A letter from my trial attorney to my POA discussing my diaries

This all boils down to the fact that the federal defender is supposed to be working for the defendant's best interests, where in fact the federal defender's work with the prosecution is in the best interests of the United States.

The defence and prosecution also work together to get the inmate to sign a plea bargain. Even if an inmate signs the plea bargain, he will then have a sentencing date on which to attend court. The plea agreement is still within the sole discretion of the sentencing judge, and the judge can still impose the maximum sentence provided by statute if he deems it necessary. In my case, that period would be five years in prison.

The plea bargain is based on a points system, and the punishment, i.e. time in prison or monetary fine, is also based on any past criminal record. My points were:

Base offence level	8
Acceptance of responsibility	– 2
Total points	= 6

In the sentencing guidelines that amount of points represented the minimum term of imprisonment of up to six months. As I had already served a period of ten weeks and three days on the day of sentencing, I was deemed 'time served', just as the guys on the inside had predicted.

My probation term was three years. Special conditions of probation were, if I was deported, excluded or allowed to voluntarily return to Britain, that I could not re-enter the United States. If I did, I would have to report to the probation officer within seventy-two hours of re-entry. Supervision would be waived upon deportation, with the exclusion of voluntary departure.

It all basically means that even though the inmate signs all conditions of the plea agreement, nothing should be taken for granted as it can all change when in front of the judge on sentencing day. As I have mentioned, in my particular case, the plea agreement that I signed had a maximum sentence of five years in prison – a bit harsh, I thought, for not being an American citizen. A fine of $250,000 also seemed a bit over the top. Then there was a court charge fee of £100. I asked my public defender on one of his visits what the £100 was for. He said he didn't know.

1

VII

2

**AGREEMENT LIMITED TO U.S. ATTORNEY'S OFFICE
SOUTHERN DISTRICT OF CALIFORNIA**

3

4   This plea agreement is limited to the United States Attorney's Office for the Southern District

5   of California, and cannot bind any other federal, state or local prosecuting, administrative, or regulatory

6   authorities, although the Government will bring this plea agreement to the attention of other authorities

7   if requested by Defendant.

8

VIII

9

APPLICABILITY OF SENTENCING GUIDELINES

10   Defendant understands the sentence imposed will be based on the factors set forth in 18 U.S.C.

11   § 3553(a). Defendant understands further that in imposing the sentence, the sentencing judge must

12   consult the United States Sentencing Guidelines (Guidelines) and take them into account. Defendant

13   has discussed the Guidelines with defense counsel and understands that the Guidelines are only advisory,

14   not mandatory, and the court may impose a sentence more severe or less severe than otherwise

15   applicable under the Guidelines, up to the maximum in the statute of conviction. Defendant understands

16   further that the sentence cannot be determined until a presentence report has been prepared by the

17   U.S. Probation Office and defense counsel and the Government have had an opportunity to review and

18   challenge the presentence report. Nothing in this plea agreement shall be construed as limiting the

19   Government's duty to provide complete and accurate facts to the district court and the U.S. Probation

20   Office.

21

IX

22

SENTENCE IS WITHIN SOLE DISCRETION OF JUDGE

23   This plea agreement is made pursuant to Federal Rule of Criminal Procedure 11(c)(1)(B).

24   Defendant understands that the sentence is within the sole discretion of the sentencing judge. The

25   Government has not made and will not make any representation as to what sentence defendant will

26   receive. Defendant understands that the sentencing judge may impose the maximum sentence provided

27   by statute, and is also aware that any estimate of the probable sentence by defense counsel is a

28   prediction, not a promise, and is **not binding on the Court**. Likewise, the recommendation made by

Def. Initials _________

5

The guidelines for sentencing

<table>
<tr>
<td>

AO 245B (Rev. 9/00) Judgment in a Criminal Case
Sheet 3 - Supervised Release

Judgment - Page _____ of _____

</td>
<td>

AO 245B (Rev. 9/00) Sentencia Final en una Causa Penal
Hoja 3 - Libertad Supervisada

Sentencia final- Página _____ de _____

</td>
</tr>
<tr>
<td>

DEFENDANT:
PHILIP MICHAEL JONES

CASE NUMBER:

</td>
<td>

ACUSADO:
PHILIP MICHAEL JONES

NUMERO DE CAUSA:

</td>
</tr>
<tr>
<td>

SUPERVISED RELEASE

Upon release from imprisonment, the defendant shall be on ~~supervised release~~ for a term of

~~Probation~~

3 years Probation

</td>
<td>

LIBERTAD SUPERVISADA

Cuando sea liberado de la penitenciaría, el acusado estará bajo libertad supervisada por un plazo de

</td>
</tr>
<tr>
<td>

MANDATORY CONDITIONS

The defendant shall report to the probation office in the district to which the defendant is released within 72 hours of release from the custody of the Bureau of Prisons unless returned to Mexico or other country of origin.

</td>
<td>

CONDICIONES OBLIGATORIAS

Si no fuere repatriado a México u otro país de origen, el acusado deberá reportarse personalmente, dentro de un plazo no mayor a 72 horas, a la oficina de libertad a prueba ubicada en el distrito en donde sea liberado de la custodia del Sistema Penitenciario.

</td>
</tr>
<tr>
<td>

The defendant shall not commit another federal, state or local crime.

</td>
<td>

El acusado no deberá cometer ningún otro delito federal, estatal o local.

</td>
</tr>
<tr>
<td>

The defendant shall not illegally possess a controlled substance.

</td>
<td>

El acusado no deberá tener en su posesión ninguna sustancia regulada en forma ilícita.

</td>
</tr>
<tr>
<td>

For offenses committed on or after September 13, 1994:
The defendant shall refrain from any unlawful use of a controlled substance. The defendant shall submit to one drug test within 15 days of release from imprisonment and at least two periodic drug tests thereafter. Testing requirements will not exceed submission of more than __4__ drug tests per month during the term of supervision unless otherwise ordered by the court.

☐ The above drug testing condition is suspended, based on the court's determination that the defendant poses a low risk of future substance abuse.

</td>
<td>

Para los delitos cometidos el 13 de septiembre de 1994 o posteriormente:
El acusado deberá de abstenerse del consumo ilícito de una sustancia regulada. Asimismo, el acusado deberá de someterse a un análisis para detectar el consumo de estupefacientes, dentro de los primeros 15 días de haber sido liberado de la penitenciaría y posteriormente a por lo menos dos análisis para detectar el consumo de estupefacientes en forma periódica. El acusado se someterá a no más de __4__ pruebas por mes durante el periodo de supervisión, a menos que el/la juez gire otra orden
☐ La condición anterior queda suspendida, con base en la determinación del juez de que existe un bajo riesgo de que el acusado se convierta en farmacodependiente en el futuro.

</td>
</tr>
<tr>
<td>

The defendant shall not possess a firearm, destructive device, or any other dangerous weapon.

</td>
<td>

El acusado no deberá tener en su posesión armas de fuego, dispositivos destructivos u otras armas peligrosas.

</td>
</tr>
<tr>
<td>

If this judgment imposes a fine or a restitution obligation, it shall be a condition of supervised release that the defendant pay any such fine or restitution that remains unpaid at the commencement of the term of supervised release in accordance with the Schedule of Payments set forth in this judgment.

</td>
<td>

Si la sentencia incluyere una multa o la obligación de pagar restitución, una de las condiciones de la libertad supervisada será que el acusado pague la multa o la restitución que aún esté pendiente de pago al inicio del plazo de libertad supervisada conforme al Plan de Pagos que se señale en la presente sentencia.

</td>
</tr>
</table>

Some of the mandatory conditions of probation

Also imposed on me were the standard conditions of a three-year probation but, as my eventual fate was deportation, probation wouldn't apply to me when in Great Britain. Probation would only apply if I was in the US. The standard conditions of probation were as follows:

1. The defendant shall not leave the judicial district without the permission of the court or probation officer.
2. The defendant shall report to the probation officer and shall submit a truthful and complete written report within the first five days of each month.
3. The defendant shall answer truthfully all inquiries by the probation officer, and follow the instructions of the probation officer.
4. The defendant shall support his or her dependants and meet other family responsibilities.
5. The defendant shall work regularly at a lawful occupation, unless excused by the probation officer for schooling, training or other acceptable reasons.
6. The defendant shall notify the probation officer at least ten days prior to any change in residence or employment.
7. The defendant shall refrain from excessive use of alcohol, and shall not purchase, process, use, distribute or administer any controlled substance or any paraphernalia related to any controlled substances, except as prescribed by a physician.
8. The defendant shall not frequent places where controlled substances are illegally sold, used, distributed or administered.
9. The defendant shall not associate with any persons engaged in criminal activity, and shall not associate with any person convicted of a felony, unless granted permission to do so by the probation officer.
10. The defendant shall permit a probation officer to visit him or her at any time at home or elsewhere and shall

permit confiscation of any contraband observed in plain view of the probation officer.

11. The defendant shall notify the probation officer within seventy-two hours of being arrested or questioned by a law enforcement officer.

12. The defendant shall not enter into any agreement to act as an informed or a special agent of a law enforcement agency without the permission of the court.

13. As directed by the probation officer, the defendant shall notify third parties of risks that may be occasioned by the defendant's criminal record or personal history or characteristics and shall permit the probation officer to make such notifications and to confirm the defendant's compliance with such notification requirement.

Mandatory Conditions of Probation

1. The defendant shall report to the probation office in the district to which the defendant is released within seventy-two hours of release from the custody of the Bureau of Prisons unless returned to Mexico or other country of origin (Great Britain).

2. The defendant shall not commit another federal, state or local crime.

3. The defendant shall not illegally possess a controlled substance.

4. For offences committed on or after September 13 1994, the defendant shall refrain from any unlawful use of a controlled substance. The defendant shall submit to one drug test within fifteen days of release from imprisonment and at least two periodic drug tests thereafter.

5. Testing requirements will not exceed submission of more than four drug tests per month during the term of supervision unless otherwise ordered by the court.

6. The defendant shall not possess a firearm, destructive device, or any other dangerous weapon.

7.   If this judgement imposes a fine or a restitution obligation, it shall be a condition of supervised release that the defendant pay any such fine or restitution obligation; it shall be a condition of supervised release that the defendant pay any such fine or restitution that remains unpaid at the commencement of the term of supervised release in accordance with the schedule of payments set forth in this judgement.

All these conditions were like having a rope around my neck for my term of probation, which was three years. I spoke to quite a few parolees who were back inside on probation violations. 78% return to prison; only 22% meet all probation requirements during the term and stay out of prison.[1] So, from the word go, the cards are stacked against a parolee. The system wants him back so that it can make more money. This is one reason why after my release I would accept deportation and not fight my case in the immigration court, which was where I was headed. It was extremely hard to give up my US life and return to Great Britain, a country that I was born into but didn't know as I had been living in the US for so many years, nearly two decades. Only with a great deal of spiritual foresight, when in MCC, did I prepare for my return to Great Britain; I was helped by friends in the US and the UK to close down my life in the States.

Every day an inmate is inside, an allocated amount of money feeds and keeps him in detainment facilities like CCA, a corporation, a money-making corporation I might add. The prison is a warehouse, and the prisoners are valuable goods in the warehouse. The US government pays CCA, as a corporation, to house inmates.

There are a wide variety of different bail systems. The granting of bail will depend on the nature of the offence and the person before the court.

Many courts fear that foreign nationals are flight risks (i.e. will leave the country and never return if granted bail). Bail is often refused in these cases. In my case, bail was set at $25,000; two people would also need to sign for the bail amount, which I had.

---

[1] According to an internal source circulating among inmates.

My attorney mentioned that he could get all the bail papers ready and I would then be released; but he also told me was there was an immigration detainer on me if released. I already knew this, as a counsellor informed me of the detainer by Immigration Customs Enforcement, or ICE. That would mean that I would be released and then detained in immigration prison until an immigration court hearing. I saw no point in doing this, even though my attorney said that he could then get my release from immigration prison for more bail. This would have been for a large fee through an associate of his who was an immigration attorney. I would have had to pay a retainer to that attorney for $1,000 and then $350 an hour. So I said thanks but no thanks and was helped through by inmates who were well versed in immigration law at MCC. I also represented myself when in immigration court.

I would also have lost time if I had been released on a sentence imposed by the federal prison system. Every day out on bail is a lost day off the sentence. So I decided to tough it out at MCC, not really knowing how long I would be in custody. I did, however, need the time to direct my power of attorney, a friend of many years, as to what to do to sell my car, close down my bank account, pay bills, file my 2005 tax returns and send my belongings and documents by ship to Great Britain. It was a complicated time, but she did a wonderful job. For that I am eternally grateful. Thank you again, Linda.

Mandatory conditions of probation are from my actual court documents. Because of these conditions, I decided not to contest my deportation in immigration court. I had continual residence in the US for over five years when I could have requested in court for an adjustment of status to permanent residence. Because of ill health at this time, I had lost 17 lb in weight, so could not endure an indefinite period of incarceration at CCA. When in front of the judge, she could see my condition and showed compassion in expediting my departure so that it was sooner rather than later.

Court Appearances

My routine every day was to get up early every morning at 4.30 a.m. to go to the bathroom, shave, and brush my teeth. In the pre-dawn light I could just about see my reflection in the plastic that was loosely called a mirror. The guys would joke that I had court every day, as I was always up so early! This is the only reason, other than the call of nature at such an early hour, why any other inmate would be up before 6 a.m.

This was also my routine at the start of a court day. My public defender would let me know from a legal visit when my next court date would be, and I made a calendar to keep a check on the dates. For such occasions, all inmates would keep one of their jumpsuits in very good condition, neatly pressed with the iron issued from the CO's office. Other inmates would also iron any inmate's jumpsuit to perfection for a Cup a Soup or piece of candy. An appointed inmate would also give free haircuts on different days for no charge, but we would usually give this guy some sort of payment, by purchasing him an item or two from the commissary shop. All this was to look our best and have a conservative haircut when appearing in front of His Honour.

We would have an early breakfast at 5.30 a.m., then wait in the common area until the elevator girl arrived to take all of us to the first stage. We would first go to a holding cell, maybe ten to twelve of us who had court that day. From that holding cell we were taken five at a time into an inspection area of five partioned cubicles in a room with a cold stone floor. There the CO would tell us all to strip off our clothes until we were naked. Humiliation didn't bother me. We then had to hold our arms out wide, open our mouths to show that there was no concealed weapon under our tongue, turn around, squat and cough so it was clear that there wasn't a concealed weapon up our rear end! The CO would examine all of our clothes wearing his gloves, then throw down the items on the floor; then we were told to get dressed.

So much for all our efforts to press our jumpsuits for court day, only to have the jumpsuit ruffled, examined and thrown down on the floor in front of us! I got annoyed about this one court day, having spent time neatly pressing my jumpsuit, so, when naked, I just waved my white arse in front of the CO when he threw my prison attire on the floor. I told all the guys later that day. They all had a laugh about that.

After dressing, we would all be herded out and they would put on our handcuffs and leg irons. We were paired up with one cuff on an inmate's right hand, and another on the left hand, and taken down in the elevator to an area at the start of a tunnel. There, we were all lined up in the tunnel. It was painted white above and orange below. We were told to face the wall with one hand on the wall and we were all frisked, just in case we had somehow managed to get a concealed weapon on our persons. Closed-circuit cameras watched our every move. Then we all started to walk down the long tunnel. It was a couple of hundred yards long under the streets of downtown San Diego across from MCC to the courthouse basement, up a flight of steps and into another holding cell. In the courthouse below we would wait until a CO came around with his clipboard calling our register number, name and what court we would appear at. There was one occasion when he came around and called out the name 'Freedom Knox'. I thought he must be kidding, and was trying to break the tension of us going to court. Nobody answered that day, and so he went on. When in medical one day, I spoke of this to a few guys, and one, to my surprise, said that he had actually met a guy by that name. How funny to have such an unusual name.

In this larger holding cell there might be forty or fifty inmates. We would then be taken in smaller numbers to another cell nearer the courtroom. There we would pace nervously. First, after having our name and register number called, we were lined up and frisked again by US marshals in the hallway, told this time to take off only our shoes, and we were patted down with clothes on, then placed in a cell to wait again. When called, we would go into the courtroom and stand by the side of our public defender with the honourable judge presiding.

During my court appearances, sometimes my public defender

would send an associate of his from his office, and only on one occasion did I ask for a continuance to appear again in court on another date as I needed time to wrap up my US life outside prison. Time was getting on, and on a legal visit my public defender said he had come to an agreement with the prosecution to inform me that a sentencing date had been set. He would then see me on that date in court.

By that time I had already signed my plea bargain, but I also informed my public defender that I had contacted the British government regarding my case.

I was 99% certain that my time would be 'time served' by my sentencing day but, just in case, I mentioned to my public defender that, should my maximum sentence of five years or any period near to that term be given, there is an agreement between the US and Great Britain that I can serve the time in a British prison and that was my request. The US government wants a defendant to sign the conditions of a plea agreement, not wanting the case to go to an expensive trial. In my case I saw no point in going to trial to contest the fact that I wasn't an American citizen, since I had handed in an application for a US passport.

This was the only charge against me.

At one court hearing I was in front of a very good judge. He mentioned that I should send the prosecution and defence some clotted cream, jam and fish and chips for their work on my case! He was hinting that I would soon be back in Great Britain, but I still had my doubts. I thanked the judge as I walked by him.

Then on 13 February 2006 I was on my way to court, going through the same routines. I hoped it would be the last court hearing as it was my sentencing day. The judge had asked for a criminal background check to be available for this day; it was, and there was no criminal background.

I had a different judge on sentencing day. He mumbled a lot and it was hard to hear what he was saying. The bailiff in front of the judge was on the phone to a government official in Great Britain and, as soon as the judge reviewed my case – giving a verdict of time served – the bailiff gave the verdict to the person on the other end of the phone. I was then asked a few questions by the court reporter from the *San Diego Union Tribune*.

I thanked the judge, and then the judge asked the probation officer in court what the probation conditions were. The lady replied that, as she understood that I was to be deported, no probation requirements were to be made other than the standard supervised release requirements, which would be issued to me. The probation term was three years.

I thanked my public defender and was then escorted back to a holding cell by a DSS agent, before being returned to my range to inform the guys of the outcome.

They were all pleased for me, and I started by give away items in my locker and returned the radio and earphones to Malcolm. The next morning I had emptied my locker, had all my prison-issued clothes ready to hand in, and was called after breakfast to leave and be discharged. I shook hands with all the guys and wished them all the best. They all cheered as I made my way to the door of freedom. Freedom was so near, yet so far away!

Plea Bargain Penalties

- A maximum of five years in prison;
- a maximum of $250,000 fine;
- a mandatory special assessment of $100; and
- a term of supervised release of three years.

Defendant understands that failure to comply with any of the conditions of supervised release may result in revocation of supervised release, requiring defendant to serve in prison all or part of the term of supervised release [i.e. if a defendant is in the wrong place at the wrong time he can and will be taken back to prison to serve a longer sentence than the original time served].

I had met many probation violees for reasons as follows: one guy visited his daughter, a violation of his probation as his probation officer told him he couldn't. An ordinary traffic stop could also place the probation violee back inside if arrested by a peace officer.

The odds are against a person on probation outlasting the term of probation with all the requirements that have to be met. One mistake and the person is back inside. The only sure way to beat all probation requirements is the drastic move to leave the US for the term of probation, and not everybody can take that pathway. However, I decided that this was the best way for me, as I never *ever* wanted to go back to prison.

The Psychological Torture of Release and Subsequent Detainment in the Space of a Day

Transfer of custody on Valentine's Day 2006

I will never forget the words of the Correctional Officer who transported me down in the MCC elevator to the booking and release area. He smugly said 'Do you know where you are going?' He knew full well that yes, I was being released from the custody of the MCC and the federal system as I was 'time served' for my crime, or as I prefer to call it 'my mistake in life'. But I knew I still wasn't free!

I already knew my destiny was to be going to CCA but for how long I didn't know. I remained silent, holding my court documents underneath my arm. At the very start of my sentence I could have got bail to be released for $25,000 and I would have needed two people to sign for the bail, and then would have been released. Not to the street I might add! I would have been released into the custody of the CCA. From the very start, I never saw the point of making bail in the federal system only to be released to the immigration system to be detained again; I would have lost time at the federal system if I had chosen to go this way. Every day out of the federal prison system is a lost day of the sentence for the crime that you are charged with and the time to serve.

Both systems wanted their pound of flesh, both at the same time! But one would have to wait. My deportation order was actually dated the day of my federal arrest date, December 2nd 2005.

On the immigration system side, if I had chosen to go this way, my public defender informed me that I would then have needed to post another bail to be released, and that amount would have been another $5,000 dollars for immigration. A total of

$30,000 for freedom, but I would still need to return to MCC for court appearances and a sentence to serve, and then appear at the immigration court for eventual deportation, which was my inevitable fate anyway.

Prisoners can have a net worth of $1,000 a day in the money markets, of all places. The cost of feeding and just keeping a prisoner alive every day to the standards that are maintained is between 75c and a few dollars a day. Prisons are warehouses, and prisoners are the goods in the warehouse. [1]

After my belongings were issued to me at MCC I was placed in a holding cell once again to await the ICE men. These are Immigration Customs Enforcement officers. Two hours later they arrived and took me into their custody. I was then placed in a holding tank, which is a larger cell with some 100 people, mainly Mexican nationals, awaiting transportation like me to CCA. The two very nice ICE men processed me and all my belongings into their system. I was interviewed by an immigration officer regarding my notice to appear in immigration court, and I stated that I would represent myself, and would like to see a judge before my deportation. He signed off the papers, I also signed, and I was then placed back in the holding cell.

The time came for transportation to CCA. I had handcuffs on both wrists and leg irons with a connecting chain from the hands to the legs. I thought that this was overkill, and trying to walk without tripping was hard. Maybe I should have fallen over; I could have sued CCA! We all made our way to the area in the parking lot beneath the building; a white bus with barred windows awaited us. Driving through the downtown streets of San Diego that I knew so well, I hoped I would have better Valentine's Days in the future than this one.

We were given a list of free immigration attorneys on the bus but, as the old saying goes, nothing is free in this life. I later found out that these so-called 'free' attorneys would charge $3,000 to $5,000 to represent you and your case.

---

[1] More information on such matters can be found at Jean Keating's website, www.wealth4freedom.com/law/prison_treatise.shtml.

File No.: ▉▉▉▉▉▉

Date: December 02, 2005

To: <u>JONES, Philip Michael</u>
(Full name of alien)

Address: <u>Otay Detention Facility, San Diego, CA 91913</u>
(Address of alien)

The Immigration and Naturalization Service has determined that you entered the United States pursuant to section 217 of the Immigration and Nationality Act. Accordingly, you executed a form I-94 W, Nonimmigrant Visa Waiver Arrival/Departure Document that explained to you the conditions of admission under the Visa Waiver Pilot Program. When you signed form I-94 W, you also waived your right to contest deportability before an immigration judge and the board of Immigration Appeals, and to any judicial review of any and all of the above decisions.

The Immigration and Naturalization Service has determined that you have violated the terms of your admission under section 217 of the Immigration and Nationality Act on the grounds that you are in violation of:

Section 237(a)(2)(A)(iii) of the Immigration and Nationality Act (Act), as amended, in that, at any time after admission, you have been convicted of an aggravated felony as defined in section 101(a)(43) of the Act.

Accordingly, the United States Immigration and Naturalization Service has entered an order that you be deported and removed from the United States.

(Signature of authorized INS official) _______________________________

Name and Title: _Meeker / ICA_

Date: _2/23/06_

Place: _ODF_

P.M. Jones
Alien acknowledgement

My deportation order, dated 2 December 2005

It was a forty-five-minute drive to CCA, which is located near Otay Mesa and the US/Mexico border. We arrived in the cold dark of night and all of the new inmates on the bus started to disembark, again trying not to fall over our chains!

CCA has a policy of running their facility under the same federal guidelines as MCC. I really think that this is, again, just so much overkill to place inmates in leg irons, and I think it is done just to try to impact on the new inmate as a scare tactic; after all, CCA is a profit-making corporation.

As we entered the facility booking area, a large – and I mean *very* large, he was about seven foot five and must have weighed at least 400 lb – African-American man greeted us. He was very polite to everybody as we had our chains removed. We again waited in the processing area for nine hours. Every person had to have a shower and a medical examination. I was tired of exams and showers, having had ten weeks and three days of medical exams and showers at MCC, so I refused. The lady CO explained that it was for my own health as some Mexican nationals have various diseases. I asked the lady if she had ever showered with thirty-seven Mexican nationals every day for ten weeks. She said no and I replied that I had, and that these Mexican nationals were very clean and disease-free. All the ten weeks that I was with them, I hadn't caught anything. She then walked off to inform her supervisor of my refusal. I also refused food as a protest, and was placed in a separate holding cell. The CO then informed me that I was to be taken to one of the units, and at about 3 a.m. I arrived at Pod P, Cell 105. I wasn't there ten minutes when I was taken back to processing as they had forgotten that I hadn't had the medical exam. So I complied and at about 4 a.m. I was placed alone in Cell 218 in Pod P, very tired. At 6 a.m., every morning, the lights in the cells came on, and the TVs in the common area outside the cells also came alive with noise – very loud, as it echoed all about.

On arrival, a new inmate is issued a standard assortment of items as follows: one plastic cup (4 oz.), a plastic spoon and fork, one plastic comb, a shower/shave liquid, a very small (3.5 in. long) toothbrush and a tube of 'Maximum Security' tooth gel. Both these last two items are supplied to CCA by Bob Barker Co. Inc.

The name is inscribed on the handle of the toothbrushes and somebody there obviously had a sense of humour in naming the toothpaste. We all assumed that this Bob Barker was the same man who hosted *The Price is Right* on CBS television. After my release I contacted the company directly to check this with them, but got no response. I was only able to retain these items since I had them with me on the day of my deportation. This was a hurried affair and no one had the opportunity to search me.

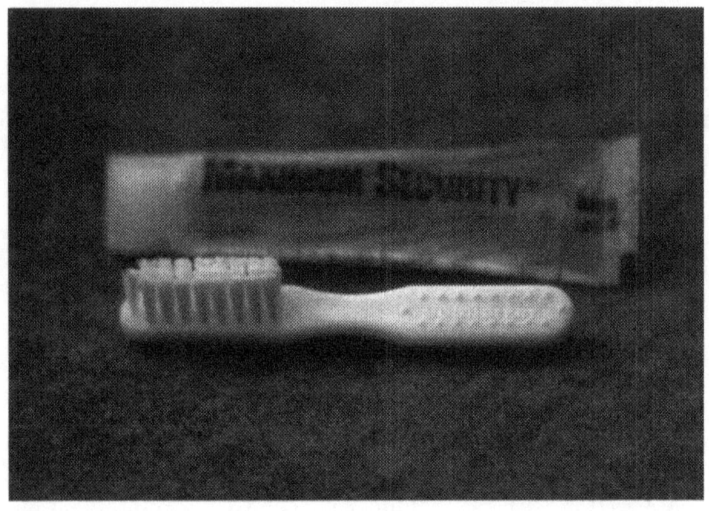

The Maximum Security toothbrush and toothpaste issued to all inmates

The same manufacturing company also supplies all CCA detainment facilities with uniforms for inmates. I was issued with my prison blues: a pair of blue pants and a blue slip-over sleeve-less shirt, a pair of elastic shower shoes, four pairs of boxer shorts, four white T-shirts, four pairs of socks and a pair of comfortable blue canvas shoes made in China. I was also given two bed sheets and one blanket. All these items were in one pillow case with two small hotel-sized square bars of soap. Also included was a blue information booklet of CCA's rules and regulations.

CCA is a well-run corporation; its aim is to maximise profit and the inmate is a valuable commodity. The facility is run under federal guidelines, with a few differences. At meal times, the inmates line up and have to give their name and cell number before receiving their food. Count time is completed with inmates in their cells, and an inmate is constantly monitored: there are cameras in the common area, hallway and the recreation yard. Permission has to be requested to even access the hallway area out of the large security doors of the area called the 'pod'. I presume that inmates were the peas in the pod! This place is maximum security

In the hallway was an assortment of books and, if available, the officer on duty would watch over an inmate's shoulder as he exchanged a book to read. Immigration request forms from the detainee to ICE could be accessed at this area, as well as medical request forms and inmate grievance forms, which could be directed to the unit manager. We also had a counsellor, a lady from the Czech Republic who did love to shout! She was a very direct person and would rarely smile; although she was a counsellor, she was rarely helpful and so inmates would only see her in her office when they were in trouble. It was like going to the headmistress' office to be caned. She didn't scare me at all and I enjoyed being called to her office when I had placed numerous grievances for various valid reasons.

She calmly explained, in one instance, that the transvestite who was placed in my cell was technically anatomically a male and that CCA was a detainment facility that housed males in separate sections to females.

Of course I understood this, but listened stern-faced to her explanation. My grievance was that CCA had placed me in the situation of sharing a cell with a transvestite, me being a hetero-sexual male all of my life. I actually had no problem with my new cellmate, but I was channelling my stress at living in an environ-ment that I had no control over; as an inmate I was constantly controlled. A person's attitude is everything and it helps to accept the facts of where you are and what you want to be; you should make the most of what is available to you. But you should not fall into a false sense of security, or forget that life is far better when you are free, and you should be working on your own case in every way, ready for your day of release, every day.

The psychology of this reasoning makes it less stressful to live in this environment. In prison, every day is the same day, like at MCC, and in time it can cause an inmate to consider suicide. I had a dream one evening that was quite vivid; I was talking to a lady and asking her the purpose of life. This lady was in spirit and not somebody that I recall from this life. As in Ecclesiastes 7:15, in my empty existence I have seen it all. This was one of the down periods that I experienced at CCA regarding the life that I had lived in the US. I had worked hard, saved, and now I felt that I was about to lose everything once I was deported. What purpose was there in continuing life? To work, live life, save and then lose everything from nearly two decades of work? Anybody reading the detainee request that I actually sent to ICE would think that I was at the point of suicide. I wasn't, but I was questioning life.

It didn't really matter what country I was living in, as this is the process of life we all live. Upon release, this frame of mind remained with me, once I had gone through everything.

The food at CCA is slopped out in portions on a plastic tray for breakfast, lunch and dinner. The food had no nutritional value, and most of the meals were very bland; some detainees would throw their share away. For dinner we would have beans, powdered potato mixed thickly into a sloppy paste, a piece of meat and jello for dessert. Breakfast would be no better, with a soup-like mixture with bits of meat, cornflakes portion, and piece of dry cake, sometimes old. Lunch was a similar type of meal.

CCA place a sex suppressant in the juice and coffee to suppress any sexual activity. My concerns were that over a longer period of time this might affect me personally. I also didn't like the fact that this was done, but can understand the reasoning behind it due to the high occurrence of rape in any prison. This is just something else an inmate has to contend with while being incarcerated, and may be an underlying reason why inmates exercise so hard to build and bulk up muscle in case of fights.

I just drank tap water, and refused the juice and coffee.

Grievance No.: ___________

Form 14-5A - For Official Use Only

CCA INMATE/RESIDENT GRIEVANCE FORM

Name (Print): JONES   PHILIP (BRITISH CITIZEN)
Last Name   First (CENSUS)   Middle Initial

Number: [redacted]   Housing Assignment: K-R 109 (FOR) ALL DETAINEES

INFORMAL RESOLUTION ATTEMPTED?   Yes ___________   No ___________

NAME OF STAFF CONTACTED ___"ATTENTION FOR THE WARDEN."___

STATE GRIEVANCE (Include documentation, witnesses, date of incident and any other information pertaining to the grievance subject. Attach additional pages if necessary).

("CCA FOOD AND NUTRITIONAL VALUE") A HIGH PERCENTAGE OF FOOD SERVED DAILY AT CCA IS COST EFFECTIVE FOR CCA, BUT OF NO TASTE (NO) OR VERY LITTLE NUTRITIONAL VALUE FOR INMATES, VERY BLAND FOOD THAT RESULTS DAILY IN A HUGE AMOUNT OF WASTE FOOD. (EXAMPLE)(MORNING) CORN FLAKES, SOME HEAT SOUP, BREAD (LUNCH) BOBOGNA AND CHEESE SANDWICH (JELLO) (DINNER) MACARONNI SOME SAME TYPE OF MEAT SMALL PIECES, PACKAGD VEGETABLES TWO COOKIES, HOLE BREAD. TO BE FAIR, SOME MEALS ARE REASONABLE, THE BALANCE IS 60 % BAD 40 % GOOD MEALS

Requested Action

(MORE WAFFLES FOR BREAKFAST, PANCAKES) MILK AT LEAST WITH 2 OR 3 MEALS (FRESH VEGETABLES) (LESS PACKAGE) VEGETABLES) MORE BEEF OR CHICKEN AT LEAST TWICE A WEEK NOT ONCE EVERY 3 WEEKS, THIS WOULD RESULT LESS WASTAGE AND STILL COST EFFECTIVE FOR CCA. MORE FRUIT DAILY. THANK YOU.

Inmate/Resident's Signature: ___PM. Jones___   Date Submitted: MARCH 8TH 06

GRIEVANCE OFFICER'S REPORT

A grievance form about the food at CCA

Diaries from 14 February 2006 to Release Date

We just got back in from the recreation yard this afternoon; we had about twenty minutes in the warm afternoon sunshine on a February afternoon. It is nice to be out in the fresh air every day, and as inmates we are lucky to go out to the yard twice a day, most days. If it is raining, we are not let out. They also give us coats if it's cold.

It's a Saturday afternoon and I'm now reading *God's Plans for You*,[1] a book here at the CCA library. It is written by J L Packer. The words of the book help me to understand how, as a Christian, a person in Christ (Romans 14:17) has energy, peace and joy every day and is inspired by the Holy Spirit. I am still ever hopeful for the uncertain future as I write. I have proved myself strong under pressure and enormous amounts of stress at MCC in this very difficult period of my life. Never once have I been discouraged, and have continued every day to do what I am inspired to do. This, I feel, was God's plan behind placing me in Metropolitan Correctional Center in San Diego, and now here at Corrections Corporation of America, hopefully for a shorter period of time than MCC. These situations were, of course, created by my own actions. A learning experience to feel, suffer as Jesus did through all who persecuted him, and for him to ask the father to forgive them, for they know not what they do.

This is what I encountered at MCC with many inmates who were also inspired by a God-given spirit never to give up, and be inspired to fight on until one day of their release. It is part of the human spirit. There are some, however, who I have encountered here at CCA who have a feeling of abandonment, and have given up on God's good graces and themselves. This I call the four 'F's – frustration, fury, failure and fear.

I came across one such person here, an English guy who had left Great Britain at the early age of six years old to come and live here

---

[1] Wheaton, IL, Crossway Books, 2001.

in the US. He has been fighting his case to stay here in the US to be with his ailing mother, but the inevitable for him will be deportation back to a country that he barely knows. I say this because the US will always deport drug offenders back to their home country and his is such a case. He shows signs of depression, desolation, disappointment and desperation every day because he hasn't got any fight left in him, having been over a year at CCA. His unwarranted bouts of anger, for the smallest incident towards either a CO or a fellow inmate, wouldn't bother the majority of people. I have tried to help this person, but he won't even help himself with the advice that I give. To know God is to have God's guidance at all times and to have the Holy Spirit speak to you in times of need. But it is also to act on what you are inspired to do, to be at peace with yourself and know that, in your hour of need, God will never forsake you in life. You will able to take on any situation that life may throw at you, and will be comforted by others who help you on your pathway in life as you should also help others.

Inmates at MCC had this faith; this English guy at CCA has lost all faith. I can only pray for him to have faith as I have, to also walk in the valley of the shadow of death, where he will fear no evil.

It's Sunday morning and I'm up early. I can't see the wall clock just outside the pod unit security doors, as the door blocks the face of the clock. My inner body clock tells me that it is about 5 a.m. I go to the bathroom, wash my hands and face, brush my teeth and brush my scalp, as I have now had my hair cut short. Usually by the time I finish my morning routine, the CO turns on the lights so I know that it must be 5.45 a.m. and I usually take about forty-five minutes to get ready as it is the one time in the morning that I like to take my time before Pamela, my cellmate, gets up. When the lights come on, the TVs also loudly wake all inmates.

When the cell door opens I usually go out to shower, as this is one of the quieter times. The water is lukewarm at best. The push button in the shower lets the water come on for forty-five seconds until you have to depress it again to get more water. This is to limit water use as CCA buys water from the city of San Diego, and CCA, of course, want to save on water usage, which costs the corporation money.

Some mornings I lie on the bed after breakfast to soak up a

few sun rays coming through the 5 in wide by 4 ft long opening called, I suppose, a window with frosted glass. As the sun moves, I also move on the fixed steel stool and table to follow its warmth as I write. Inside the cell, as in every cell, is a metal toilet with no seat that is connected to the handbasin above. A little water spout is operated for the lukewarm water; when the button is depressed cold water comes on for six seconds. There is also a flush button on the unit at the right side.

When sitting on the pot, you are so close that you could actually pat your fellow inmate's head as he lies head-first towards you. The proximity was not easy to get used to while going to the bathroom any day.

The Mexicans I share with always seem to sleep with their head pointing towards the cell door; I sleep with my feet pointing towards the cell door.

My cellmate, Pamela, acts like a typical woman in front of the mirror, as he brushes his long blonde hair. Even though he goes to medical to have his female hormone injections, he still shaves the hair that grows on the back of his hands daily. His given name is Mario, but he prefers to be called Pamela. He is a pleasant person and has two little babies in Costa Mesa, California. One day he showed me the pictures. I presume that the babies are adopted, and I didn't enquire as to who was his partner, male or female. My Spanish is limited.

There are now three people in Pod R who are transvestites. Besides Pamela, with whom I share a cell, there is Maria from San Salvador, next door, who is asking for political asylum and has been at CCA for nine months. Also Alexandria, from Tijuana. He also has long, dark brown hair past his shoulders, all real hair, just like Pamela.

Maria has short black hair tied in a bun at the back of his head. He rolls his 'r's in appreciation, as he fancies another inmate in another unit; this guy's name is China, who has a powder keg of a personality. He often takes off his ID band and disobeys authority, so is sent back to his pod unit with no meals. Not that it is such a bad thing, due to the poor quality of some of the meals at CCA; they barely keep everybody alive. George in Pod P complains

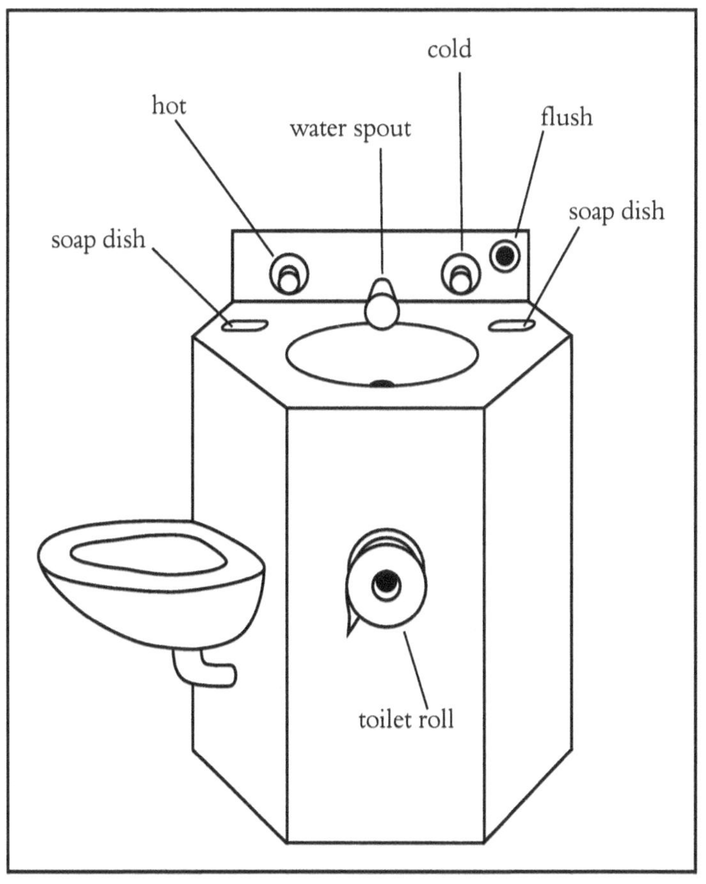

Diagram of washbasin and metal toilet (no seat) in the cells at CCA

daily, and justly so, about the food, which has no nutritional value.

For breakfast we had a piece of old bread, some mushroom soup with bits of some sort of meat, grits and a piece of cornbread cake. Lunch was no better, with shredded cabbage, a little dressing on the cabbage, then beans, a slice of bologna, two pieces of a cake that was also old, and of course the mandatory chocolate jello. Meals like this have very few calories and CCA is a great place to come to lose weight and beats any Jenny Craig or Weight Watchers scheme.

There is, of course, sexual innuendo as I share a cell with Pamela. When Manuel, an eighteen-year-old boy from Tijuana, came to my cell for a few days, he was moved as he was placed in a 'boat' in my cell due to no room. This is a plastic container with two mattresses to make up a crowded situation in a two-bunk cell that is 4 ft wide by 12 ft long. It is a violation of our human rights to be so overcrowded; it was unsanitary and dangerous if I fell over Manuel. Next day I placed a grievance to the unit manager stating this, and was taken by the manager to his office so he could contest my grievance. After I met him in his office, the very next day all boats were removed from four cells, not only mine, and this is where Manuel was moved out and Pamela moved in. As a heterosexual male, it didn't bother me and actually brought a smile to my face to see Pamela walk in. I thought that things couldn't get any better for that book that I am writing.

Even though I also put in another grievance for having to share a cell with a transvestite male, my objection was that this could psychologically damage me for the rest of my life because CCA placed me and this person in this situation. I totally respect Pamela as a person, and Pamela respects me. In fact my power of attorney, Linda, was surprised when I called her with a request to help Pamela. This request for was for Linda to phone Pamela's sister as she had no idea where he was, and I knew the system well enough to inform Pamela that he would have a court date to appear in seven to ten days, and then would serve a minimum detainment period of thirty days depending on his case. Pamela wasn't very happy to learn this, and as he couldn't make the collect call to his sister's cell phone, I asked Linda to make the call for Pamela. It was just to inform his sister of where he was and for his sister to send some money as he had very little on him when arrested at the border. He couldn't contact his relatives through the very expensive phones. These phones charged $4 for the first minute and $2 for every other minute; another way in which CCA exploited inmates. My calls to my power of attorney averaged $7 to $10 for a few minutes. Again, it was true that wealth could be exchanged for freedom. All calls were monitored as well. Because of this incident, Pamela and I have a mutual respect for each other.

Pamela was quite concerned for me when I went on a hunger strike for a few days. I have put in grievances about the food at CCA and tried to ask other inmates to back me up. But there is such apathy here; inmates continually complain to me and each other about the low standard of food served, but when they have a chance to do something, and put their name to the grievance as well, they all decline. So I did it alone. One inmate said, 'Just put on your grievance: "from all inmates"!' That's an easy way out for me to take all the heat! Another said that CCA could claim that I was trying to incite a riot, so they wouldn't sign. I survived on a few packets of nuts that were high in protein and a vitamin C powdered drink that I had purchased from commissary. COs at CCA couldn't care less if you eat or not. If you line up at meal times and say your name and cell number they can tick you off the list as having a meal; if you don't turn up, they simply don't record you as having eaten and that's it!

After a few days of my self-imposed hunger strike I went out for a breakfast of powdered eggs, two pieces of stale bread, some grits (semolina) made with water, a small milk and piece of cake. Oh! It was so good to eat again. The counsellor told me today that my request to be moved back to Pod P where I was before coming to Pod R had been denied. That didn't surprise me as I also put in a lot of valid grievances when in Pod P. I think I was moved because in Pod P I had some very interesting heated conversations with Riddic from Croatia, and George. We all got on so well and enjoyed talking about so many topics; the constant cameras that observed our every move perhaps caught the eye of a CO or unit manager who thought it best we be split up. As I got to know how to play the system, maybe they felt that they didn't know what do with me. As one inmate commented to me, I have always been a fighter in spirit, and I was causing a lot of paperwork for the unit manager who had to respond to my grievances and write up a report for the warden.

I think this helped me to get an early release from detainment!

A drawing by my eighteen-year-old cellmate at CCA,
with the mind of a child

Grievance No.: 06-049   Form 14-5A - For Official Use Only

CCA INMATE/RESIDENT GRIEVANCE FORM

Name (Print): JONES   PHILIP
Last Name   First   Middle Initial

Number: [redacted]   Housing Assignment: K - R - 109

INFORMAL RESOLUTION ATTEMPTED?   Yes ________   No ________

NAME OF STAFF CONTACTED ________

STATE GRIEVANCE (Include documentation, witnesses, date of incident and any other information pertaining to the grievance subject. Attach additional pages if necessary).

"ILLEGAL" OVERCROWDING IN CELL, A VIOLATION OF MY HUMAN RIGHTS. I HAVE INFORMED THE BRITISH GOVERNMENT. THESE CONDITIONS ARE VERY UNSANITORY AND DANGEROUS, I COULD FALL AND INJURY COULD HAPPEN. I HOLD CCA RESPONSIBLE.

Requested Action
DEPORTATION IMMEDIATELY ALL TRAVEL DOCUMENTS ARE HERE AT CCA. I HAVE SIGNED MY "INTENT TO REMOVE".

Inmate/Resident's Signature: P.M.Jones   Date Submitted: 3/5/2006

GRIEVANCE OFFICER'S REPORT

GRIEVANCE OFFICER'S DECISION
At times we are forced to triple bunk on a temporary basis. During this time each detainee should take special care to ensure their area is clean. Also, care should be given to safety to avoid any unsafe practice by estimates.

Grievance Officer's Signature: ________   Date: 3-13-06

Inmate/Resident's Signature (upon request): ________   Date: ________

APPEAL: Yes ________   No ________   STATE REASON (S) FOR APPEAL: ________

WARDEN/ADMINISTRATOR'S RESPONSE

Warden/Administrator's Signature: ________   Date: ________
Inmate/Resident's Signature (upon request): ________   Date: ________

Revised 02/01/02

A grievance form about cell overcrowding

Free as Birds… or are they?

I was surprised to see two little sparrows fly around in Pod P where I was first before being moved to Pod R. Inmates say that when the CCA facility was built about five years ago the two birds came and stayed.

They both flew around freely, especially when all inmates were under lockdown. Inmates would cut off the bottom of a milk carton to fill with water for the birds, and put out cake, nuts or bread daily for them. They both seemed to survive quite well, probably better than they would do in the wild. When the temperature in the pod area was hotter, one bird was on the floor seemingly having suffered from the heat. An inmate gave the bird a drink of milk and threw it up in the air. It took off and flew to the safety of its mate. The next day all seemed well with both birds.

I think that those two little birds gave hope to the inmates that one day they might be free. The birds had adjusted to being incarcerated, and made no attempt to fly out the door when it was open, or fly into the large glass windows that separated the inside of Pod P from the hallway.

Stress levels are much lower when a person inside accepts their circumstances. While at CCA I never came to the point in my mind of accepting being there. In the recreation yard, when caged like an animal in the zoo, I paced back and forth as the guard watched my movements. I was exhibiting signs of anxiety and stress; but I wasn't stressed inside, I was quite calm.

Closed-circuit cameras would watch our every move inside the unit and outside in the yard. We all were performing on a stage for the guards and COs; they were our audience every day. The two little birds accepted their existence of where they were, but I never would. I think that this inner strength and defiance helped me to leave the facility sooner rather than later.

Asylum Seekers

I question what is wrong with humanity that it incarcerates people who are only looking for a better way of life than what they had or didn't have in their own country. This is why they came to the United States. CCA is a corporation that makes money from human suffering, keeping people caged up like animals every day. It is such a loss of human life to be kept this way, sometimes for years. We live in the twenty-first century, in a world of technology in the most powerful country in the world, and this is the best solution the US can come up with for people. The crimes that people commit should be punished, especially drug crimes that cause so much misery for families, but if there wasn't the demand, there would be no need for the supply. A lot of asylum seekers just came to the US for a better life. I spoke to a group in the yard one day and, having lived in San Diego for nineteen years, I was trying to give them all an honest perspective of what life could lie ahead for them. San Diego is indeed America's finest city, and I was hoping for them all to get an 'adjustment of status' to eventually be released into America, to live the American dream.

I will always speak positively in every way of San Diego, as it has been a wonderful experience for me to live here for all these years. It will be such a fantastic adventure for all these people to embark on a life in San Diego, and they should all give the life here a chance.

They all couldn't have chosen a better city to start their new lives, and I am excited for them. It was good to see the anticipation in their eyes as I told them stories of my life in San Diego, especially Sharif from Iraq. The United States is indeed a wonderful country with many opportunities and rewards for hard work.

I have lived my life here as a citizen, even though the United States only recognises me as an alien. It doesn't matter, as I know who I am: a person who has lived here as a law-abiding citizen, a person of good moral character; a person who came to the US for a better way of life and found it for nearly two decades.

Another such person is Ayan, whom I met while at CCA. He is from a small village in the Afgooye region of Somalia and is a member of the Darot tribe.

The Hawiye tribe were at war with the Darot,[1] so Ayan's family decided that he should leave for a better life in Kenya, and from there go to America. It took Ayan seven years to finally get to America.

He is a young boy of about nineteen, but he looks older. He has a good command of English, having been taught by a man who went around villages in Kenya. While there, Ayan sold cigarettes on the streets and in a shop where, in a few years, the owner paid him enough for his air fare to Mexico City. This shop owner was also a people trafficker with contacts in Mexico. From Mexico City, all alone, Ayan took to the bus to Tijuana to go to a contact. There he was given a false California licence with a picture of an African man who looked nothing like Ayan. He then made his way to the US/Mexico border and told the immigration officers to arrest him as he was claiming political asylum, having travelled from Somalia. He only had a few dollars left in his pocket when he crossed into the United States; it had taken him several years to get from Kenya.

On the same subject, a book called *Coming Home: The Experience of Enlightenment in Sacred Traditions* by Lex Hixon[2] (foreword by Ken Wilber) was in the CCA library. I read chapter eight by Bawa Muhaiyadeen, who came from the jungles of Sri Lanka. One day I sat down to have a meal with three very polite lads from Sri Lanka, who had been held at CCA for four years and four months. Their cases were at Supreme Court level. They all finished their meal before me, but stayed seated until I had completely finished. The US was investigating these young lads to the fullest extent, and it was hard for me to comprehend how they had survived at CCA for such a long period. They seemed well adjusted, would all play basketball in the yard, with quite

---

[1]   See   www.amnestyusa.org/countries/somalia/index.do   for   more information on the plight of many Somali refugees. I received similar information from my cellmate Ayan at CCA.

[2] New York, Larson Publications, 1978.

happy dispositions, and had resigned to the control of the system.

I didn't know the exact situations of their court cases, but I suspect that they were being held at CCA as suspect terrorists. I came to this conclusion because political asylum seekers are released to the US streets in a matter of months, as with Sharif from Iraq. He contacted me while living in San Diego to inform me he was so happy to be free.

Deportation Day, Day of Release Rush

I expected to be taken from my cell in the very early hours of the morning, which was the usual pattern for inmates who were going to be deported.

In the morning at around 5.30 a.m., I overheard two COs talking, and one Filipino officer said to the other, 'Cancellation of removal', adding that you can't talk to a unit manager and counsellor like I did. I always showed respect when speaking in the counsellor's office or talking to the unit manager, so I was surprised at this. My complaints were valid and justified; but I made it clear that I wouldn't accept being at CCA and had put in numerous complaints about the food, my sharing a cell with a transvestite, being held at CCA against my will as all travel documents were already prepared for my deportation, etc. In fact, my deportation order was actually for the very day that I was arrested; I had been placed in MCC and served a sentence of ten weeks and three days that I should never have served, and I should have just been deported on that very day in December of 2005. But this is how the judicial system works, and the federal system wanted to punish me and also to make money from my incarceration.

Hearing the officers' conversation set me thinking. Perhaps they were going to tag on another thirty days at CCA – that thought really depressed me. Then at 6 a.m. that morning the CO said that I had to go to medical again. I had already been to medical the day before for a check-up and exam, so I couldn't understand why I was going again. I waited and waited as usual, then eventually saw the doctor. It seemed that as I had written him so many long medical requests, he basically just wanted to have a chat with me. We talked about everything from London to Paris, and even him writing a book about all his work at CCA. I thanked him and left to return to the Pod R unit, encouraged by my talk with the good doctor. Maybe the talk was just to see if I was psychologically OK to travel.

At lunch I was with Ayan, my friend from Somalia. He had had good news at his court case that day and he needed to find a lawyer in two weeks for his asylum case. We were then placed under lockdown after lunch, and I was going to the toilet when a voice came over the intercom in the cell. The voice said, 'Philip Jones.' I said, 'Yes, sir.' He then said, 'Wait a minute,' and came back saying, 'You have to get ready to go *now*!'

I came out of the cell, as I wanted to shower before my travel. Both officers on duty said, '*No!*' as I started to walk up the steel steps to the upper shower.

'*You need to go now; get all your stuff ready!*' they shouted.

I was escorted to the booking and receiving area, handed in my CCA items of clothing and bedding and was given my personal clothes and belongings. I changed as quickly as I could, signed my release papers, which were placed in front of me, signed for what money I had and then, before I knew it, I was in the van with the ICE officers. We drove through the razorwire-topped gates. CCA: a place that I never looked back on as we drove out. We headed on to Interstate 805 North to Los Angeles. *LA?* I thought. *Why not San Diego Airport, just a short drive away?* I asked the officers and one replied that I was departing from LA, hence the need to drive at 80 mph plus! The urgency was to get to LAX so I would be on the flight to London in time, and to try and beat the rush hour in LA. We left at about 2 p.m. and thankfully arrived safe at LAX at around 5 p.m. with enough time to pick up the one-way boarding pass, from the check-in counter.

Curbside at LAX one ICE officer asked me if he had to cuff me. I replied, 'No sir.' Then he said that I should stay close to him and follow him. He stayed ahead, directing me at all times while the other officer walked behind me.

When he was getting my boarding pass, I noticed he only had one. So I asked the other officer behind me if he ever had to accompany a person on a deportation flight.

He replied, 'Only if you were an aggravated felon. You are not, are you?'

I then said that I was just asking and kept my silence. After that, we made our way to the departure lounge, and both officers observed the area to pick a place to sit. We made our way to an

JONES/PHILIP MICHAEL   DEPU   07Mar06   12:16pm

Booking locator: MHGHYZ
Fare: $239.50

16Mar06   07:05pm   Thursday
Air   American Airlines   Flight# 136   Class:W Seat:41F
       From: Los Angeles CA, USA   16Mar06   07:05pm   Thursday
       To: London Heathrow EN, U 17Mar06   01:25pm   Friday
       Meal: Dinner Breakfast Equip: Boeing 777 Jet Status: Confirmed
       Stops: 0

       DEP-TERMINAL 4   ARR-TERMINAL 3
       ONEWORLD
       American Airlines locator: MHGHYZ

DOCUMENT ENVELOPE CHECK-OFF LIST.

1. TD & I-94
2. TICKET OR GTR
3. DOCUMENT OF AUTHORITY (I-205, I-274 (A), ETC.
4. TRANSFER ARRANGEMENTS (I-216, I-380, G-391, DATYJ & DAZAS.

My deportation itinerary

enclosed four-seat section, where both officers sat, one to my left and one directly in front of me. One got up to have a walk around, and answer a personal call on his cellphone. The other, a grey-haired chap of around sixty (with eighteen years of service with ICE) started to nod off to sleep. It must have been a long day for him, so I started a conversation. He had about five more years to work before retirement, and I asked him about his experiences on the job. By this time the other officer had come back and joined in the conversation.

Both officers were very cordial and polite. At the Mexican/US border where they often patrolled, the Mexican Nationals on their side would throw rocks at the ICE men. The officers could only return fire by way of pepper pellets at the border crossers. Both officers had holstered .40 calibre revolvers that they were ready to use in any self-defence situation. It seemed to me that both officers seemed to trust me as I was well behaved, and I really had no intention of making a move to escape their custody. I must admit, though, that if I had wanted to, it would have been easy to go through the far double-door exit point, down to the area where the planes were, like Bruce Willis did in one of his movies.

I was actually getting quite anxious to be on the plane due to my conversation down at the check-in area with the older officer. It wasn't too long before the flight to London (non-stop, of course) had arrived, and we started to make our way through the departure gate. Again, one led and one walked behind me. I could see from the other passengers' looks that they were bemused and curious as to why two officers were escorting me on to the plane.

It was quite fun and so good to be free!

The first officer talked to the cabin crew, explained who I was and handed over my passport and travel documents. He explained to me that, upon my landing at London Heathrow, my British passport would then be handed to me. I remained calm, but was very excited to be on the plane at last, even though all I had with me to show for nineteen years of living in the US were my court documents with the diaries of everything that had happened to me in the past few months written on the back. This was the only way to get any information out of either prison. I thanked both officers as they left me, and asked if the first would like the number of a Ferrari car dealer that he could hire to drive one weekend in La Jolla. He was an expert driver and I thought it would be fun for him to do this one weekend with either his girlfriend or wife (I didn't know if he was married). He thanked me and took the number. I then also thanked the other officer and shook his hand, and wished him the best in life. Then I made my way to my seat, 41F, on the plane to London.

Back in Great Britain

When we arrived on British soil at Heathrow Airport, all the passengers were still seated when the stewardess came up to me with the envelope that had my British passport enclosed. She had a stern look on her face; she never uttered a word, just handed me the envelope, said nothing, and walked off. I said, 'Thank you', as she headed off back to the exit door to say goodbye to passengers.

The document envelope had instructions on the front to the stewardess:

> Please do not place these documents in the hands of any alien concerned.

My name and alien number were noted below. Then, below that, also on the front of the envelope was:

> Please give this envelope to an Immigration Officer of this service, or of the government of the country to which destined, who will meet the plane upon arrival and take custody of the alien. [Sounds like I came from another planet.] If the flight is terminated in the United States, short of the schedule's destination [just to cover all events!], please turn the alien over to the local police authorities and ask them to call this office [no office number noted!] or the nearest office of the Immigration and Naturalization Service, call collect.

The cost of my flight was $239.50, one-way of course. Quite a deal, I thought, for an American Airlines flight from Los Angeles to London Heathrow on a Boeing 777 jet. No stops, of course, and I was not met by any immigration officer when on British soil; I just had a warm smile from the immigration officer and was welcomed back to the UK as I walked through British customs and immigration!

Life after Prison: Psychological, Emotional and Physical

The after-effects of prison still linger on into my life in everyday society. I still wake in the very early hours of the morning, only this time I hear the dawn chorus of the birds singing before sunrise. This exchange is a lot better than the constant loud snoring of many inmates or the clang of steel doors. It is difficult to adjust to life, not really knowing what purpose or position one now has to establish.

I still look to every day that I am free with anticipation and excitement, and I have faith that everything will work out. It will take a lot of hard work, researching, meeting people, phone calls and travelling to places for me to eventually have a place to rest my head that I can call home. Just having a roof over my head is a start and being able to walk free on the streets in the rain or sun, in the day or night of any town or city is such a wonderful feeling. I just have to pick up the pieces of life and carry on.

People on the outside also prejudge people who are incarcerated. I can understand in some ways how a person on the outside wouldn't want any contact with an inmate. I asked friends on the outside, who have known me well over the years, to carry out some requests for me. They refused, and I respect their decision. What I wanted to achieve was to only place some small amounts, $50 each, in commissary accounts for the inmates who were a tremendous amount of help to me. I took care of this when I was finally released. Smith, who works for 60c a day, getting up at 5 a.m. to go work in the kitchens of MCC (eight hours a day), earning $14.40 (£7 estimate) a month was one person I wanted to help.

I am happy to have been able to do this for the guys that are still inside. They can now buy some comfort food every week.

Release and Resettlement

One day, gone will be the poor excuse for food slopped out on plastic trays three times a day. Gone will be the lukewarm showers that spray for thirty-five seconds, forcing you to push the button again for the water to come back on. Taking a shower when it is cold, you tend not to linger for more than a few minutes. Gone will be the visits to the recreation yard with the coils of razor wire and the 30 ft high fences between the inmate and the view to freedom that we can see in the distance every day, so near, yet so far away. Gone will be the familiarity of getting to know fellow inmates, before you are moved to another pod and cell. Change is constant in the universe, and change is ever-present in the prison system at CCA. Somehow, some way, a person in this environment has to find the strength to go on. No matter what our crimes, we are all still human beings, not aliens from another planet.

Only my faith in God kept me going, providing me with the inspiration to prepare for the life after my release.

I played the system as the system played and detained me. My only crime was that I wasn't a citizen, but under the true definition, I was. I had lived in the city of San Diego for nineteen years as a law-abiding state and federal taxpayer.

I feel a deep sense of sadness and gratitude that I was able to live in the US all those years. It is indeed a wonderful country.

The day of my release couldn't have come quickly enough for me and I felt the day drawing near. This would be a rebirth; I celebrated by having my head shaved. Due to the conformity of society, this can only really be done when inside, where the look is accepted; not in the real world, where there have to be different standards. Fortunately my hair grew in a matter of months, so it was back to an acceptable style for society when I returned. I am still very exhausted, and will need a lot of rest now I am back in Great Britain. Prison takes everything out of you every day, physically, mentally and emotionally. I have had to take time to contemplate and release all feelings of my experience before moving on in life to be a productive person in society, as we have all been programmed to be in life. I must now hold down a job, find a place to live, pay bills, build a structured social life; all this is hard to do after being in a prison environment. It makes me wonder what the meaning of life is.

Is it all worth it to come back to this existence? Suicide comes to mind as an easier option out than having to deal with everyday life after such a controlled existence in prison. Psychological healing is needed, which hopefully will come in time. Every day in the recreation yard I would do thirty push-ups and pace back and forth along sections of the wire fence, feeling like a caged animal. I would envision a white tiger in my mind's eye, waiting and looking for a release. You can usually tell the ones who have resolved to be in this existence and the ones who work out hard, who do not accept their existence in prison. Looking for the day of freedom, so many Mexicans cross the border to come to the 'CCA hotel' every day. These are the ones who like the food and the life there, so the constantly revolving door between Mexico and the US will continue. I wonder if, one day, this will all end; will there be open borders, as in Europe? I think not, as the US wouldn't make so much money.

There should also be a better support system from central and local government for a person coming back into a country, and eventually society, after a prison sentence. Somebody to talk to, who understands, would help to prepare people to handle the pressures of living that we all endure, every day, instead of the couldn't-care-less attitude that sometimes exists. I hope this book will inspire changes to be made in the future.

Social Psychology of Work

Life is never perfect, but we should all be thankful that we have our lives to live on earth.

Society and governments have conditioned us to get a job, pay taxes, work hard – for what? To pay bills and exist!

I did this in Great Britain for years, and then in the US for many more years, and could have lost everything that I worked hard for over nearly two decades.

I have returned to my birth country, although America was my home, with a bunch of court documents underneath my arm to show for all this life. Is it all worth it?

We all need to work to survive, but money doesn't make you happy. Finding a purpose in life is the aim of our never-ending quest. We should live with no regrets, through the ups and downs, twists and turns that life throws our way. We can handle the challenges that come our way; the power of the human spirit is never-ending until the day of passing on. Every person can use their God-given talents and abilities in life to help each other. If we all make this effort, this world in which we all live will be a better place.

Thank you all for buying and reading this book.

Postscript

Prisoners Abroad

Prisoners Abroad are based in Font Hill Road, London. I contacted them when I was at MCC in San Diego and they sent me an information package.

When I arrived at Heathrow Airport, I phoned the freephone number at Prisoners Abroad and spoke to Theresa, my case worker. From the very start at the airport, and back in a country that I really didn't know as I had been in America for so many years, I received a tremendous amount of help and guidance from Theresa. Also Travel Care at the airport were of great help, especially Jean.

Case workers at Prisoners Abroad are extremely helpful; they understand what a person has gone through in prison, and know that person still faces the many challenges of everyday life.

Some of the proceeds of this book will go to Prisoners Abroad and Travel Care so they can continue their work for other expats returning to Great Britain.

Hello and welcome to our first newsletter of 2006. We hope to be making some big changes to the newsletter over the course of the year, which should make it a more bright and interesting read. If you have any suggestions on how we could improve, we're always interested to hear from you, so please write in to the usual address.

In this issue we have several accounts of events that led to people being sent to prison. We also have an article from a Consul in Ecuador, as a late entry in our "Day in the Life" submissions. We also have a useful piece from the wife of a prisoner in France about her experience of prison visiting. We'd be interested in hearing more opinions on visiting, and the impact a visit can have – so please write in with your thoughts to the address on the front page.

As always, my thanks go to all the contributors, and also to all those who wrote pieces which couldn't be included this time. We receive many letters, and unfortunately it's not possible to include everything.

Stephen

I was born in a small village in Wales, Great Britain, and arrived in California on August 1st 1987. In just one month I got myself a job, a car and a place to live, as I was determined to live the American Dream. Over the following years I had various jobs, including at a cable TV company, a retirement home and a Cancer Research Institute. This institute was the place of my arrest. The crime that I was charged with was regarding my application for a US passport. The charge was later dropped, but I have now been charged with stating that I was a US citizen on the application. I truly felt that as I had lived in the US as a person of good moral character, with no criminal record in 19 years (not even a parking ticket) that I was a citizen. In all the years that I have lived here I have paid state and federal taxes, and filed tax returns every year.

Why did I apply for a US passport, when I already had a valid, up-to-date UK passport? The one and only reason was to secure my future retirement here in the US. I have paid into the social security system, as a lot of Americans have, so I was only trying to secure my future here in the same way. To now lose all that I have worked for in two decades is just not right! I accept the mistake that I made, and these past months in prison I feel that I have paid restitution not only with my time, but my health which has suffered. I'm in a holding prison, and even though the inmates are well looked after, prison is still prison.

PJ, USA

My letter appearing in Prisoners Abroad News, Vol 17, Issue 1, Spring 2006, p. 2.

And may the God of hope fill you with all joy and
peace by your faith in him, until, by the power of the
Holy Spirit, you overflow with hope.

Romans, 15:13 (NEB)